STEP-BY-STEP WRITING

A STANDARDS-BASED APPROACH

Linda Lonon Blanton

HEINLE
CENGAGE Learning·

Australia • Brazil • Japan • Korea • Mexico • Singapore • Spain • United Kingdom • United States

HEINLE
CENGAGE Learning·

Step–By–Step Writing: A Standards–Based Approach, Book 3
Linda Lonon Blanton

Publisher: Sherrise Roehr

Associate Development Editor: Catherine McCue

Director, US Marketing: Jim McDonough

Senior Product Marketing Manager: Katie Kelley

Content Project Manager: John Sarantakis

Print Buyer: Susan Carroll

Composition: Pre-Press PMG

Cover Design: Silber Design

© 2009 Heinle, Cengage Learning

> For permission to use material from this text or product, submit all requests online at **cengage.com/permissions**
> Further permissions questions can be emailed to **permissionrequest@cengage.com**

Library of Congress Control Number: 2007932076

ISBN-13: 978-1-4240-0402-7
ISBN-10: 1-4240-0402-0

Heinle
20 Channel Center Street
Boston, MA 02210
USA

Cengage Learning is a leading provider of customized learning solutions with office locations around the globe, including Singapore, the United Kingdom, Australia, Mexico, Brazil, and Japan. Locate your local office at: **international.cengage.com/region**

Cengage Learning products are represented in Canada by Nelson Education, Ltd.

Visit Heinle online at **elt.heinle.com**
Visit our corporate website at **cengage.com**

Printed in the United States of America
2 3 4 5 6 7 8 9 10 — 12 11 10 09

ACKNOWLEDGMENTS

Heinle would like to thank the following consultants and reviewers:

Consultants

Jennifer Runner
Atwater High School
Atwater, California

Alicia Bartol-Thomas
Sarasota County Schools
Sarasota, Florida

Patricia Levine
Colts Neck High School
Colts Neck, New Jersey

Vivian K. Kahn
Halsey Intermediate School 296
New York City Dept. of Education
Brooklyn, New York

Reviewers

Teresa Arvizu
McFarland Unified School District
McFarland, California

M. Danielle Bragaw
Bedichek Middle School
Austin, Texas

Gary Bechtold
New Boston Pilot Middle School
Dorchester, Massachusetts

Maria Celis
Lamar High School
Houston, Texas

Linda Contreras
Luther Burbank High School
Sacramento, California

Susannah Courand
T.C. Williams High School
Alexandria, Virginia

Dana Dusbiber
Luther Burbank High School
Sacramento, California

Sara Farley
Wichita High School East
Wichita, Kansas

Sharolyn Hutton
Newcomer School
Ontario, California

Barbara Ishida
Downey High School
Modesto, California

Dana Liebowitz
Palm Beach Central High School
Wellington, Florida

Barbara M. Linde
YorkTown, Virginia

Andrew Lukov
School District of Philadelphia
Philadelphia, Pennsylvania

Jennifer Olsen
Chiefess Kamakahelei Middle
    School
Lihue, Hawaii

Mary Susan Osborn-Iratene
Will Rogers Middle School
Fair Oaks, California

Diana Sefchik
North Plainfield High School
North Plainfield, New Jersey

Malgorzata Stone
Franklin High School
Seattle, Washington

Alison Tepper
Western Middle School
Greenwich, Connecticut

Mark Trzasko
Okeeheelee Middle School
West Palm Beach, Florida

Karin VonRiman
Abraham Clark High School
Roselle, New Jersey

Deborah Wilkes
Lee County High School
Sanford, North Carolina

Clara Wolfe
William Allen High School
Allentown, Pennsylvania

TABLE OF CONTENTS

TO THE STUDENT

How to use this book

Pre-Reading
Look at images related to the reading. Analyze the images to learn about a topic before reading about it.

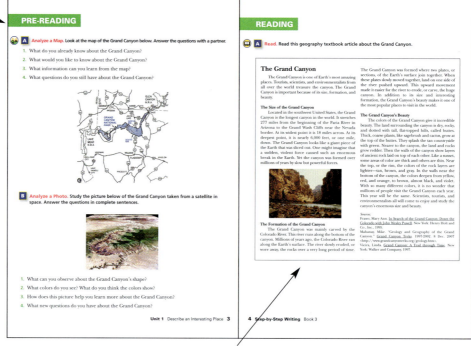

Read
Read a short passage. This models new language you can use for your writing.

Vocabulary
Practice the words you need.

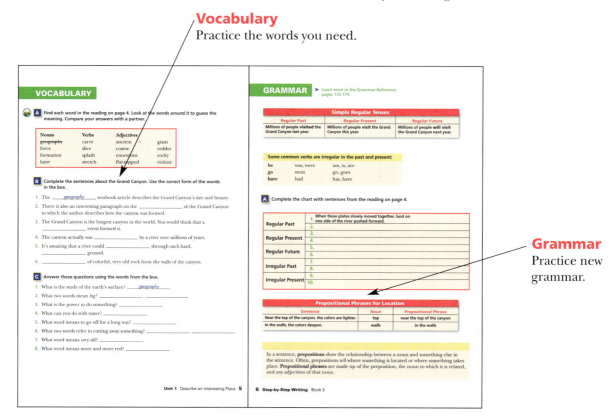

Grammar
Practice new grammar.

Remember!
Learn language points and ways to improve your writing.

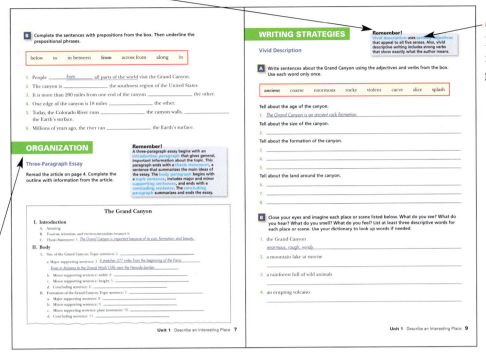

Organization
Practice ways to organize information.

Glossary Terms
Learn more about new words in the glossary on pages

Writing
See a model of a student's writing. This helps you understand your goal.

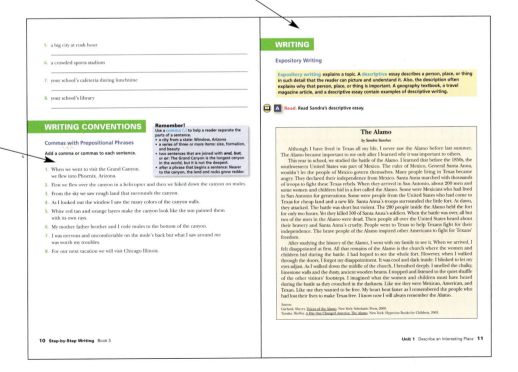

Strategies / Conventions
Practice making your sentences and paragraphs clear and correct.

Writing Prompt
Read the writing prompt. This tells you what to do.

Step 1: Pre-write
Look at model notes and a graphic organizer. Then you think of ideas and take notes.

Step 2: Organize
You put your ideas in order. This will help the reader to understand your writing.

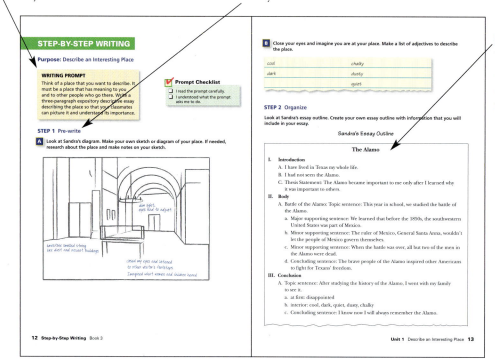

Step 3: Draft and Revise
Look at a model first draft and make corrections. Then you write your own first draft. You think of how to improve your writing. Then you revise your writing.

Step 5: Publish
Make a final draft of your writing. Now you can share it with your class or your family.

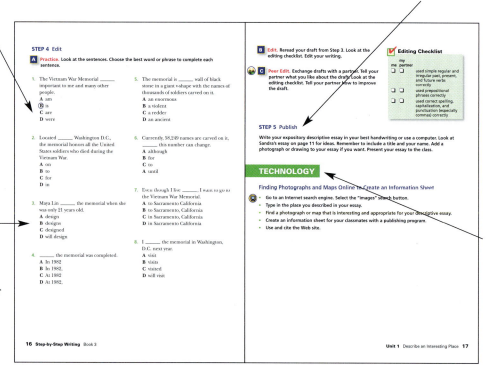

Step 4: Edit
Find errors in model sentences and correct them. Then, you edit your own draft. In Peer Edit, exchange drafts with a partner. Then make suggestions for improvement.

Technology
Use a computer to find and format new information.

PHOTO CREDITS

Unit 1

Describe an Interesting Place

UNIT OBJECTIVES

Writing
expository writing

Organization
three-paragraph essay
spatial order

Writing Strategies
vivid description

Writing Conventions
commas with prepositional
  phrases

Vocabulary
sensory adjectives

Grammar
simple past, present,
  and future tenses
prepositional phrases
  for location

Technology
finding a photograph or map
  online
creating an information sheet

Grand Canyon

A **Analyze a Map.** Look at the map of the Grand Canyon below. Answer the questions with a partner.

1. What do you already know about the Grand Canyon?

2. What would you like to know about the Grand Canyon?

3. What information can you learn from the map?

4. What questions do you still have about the Grand Canyon?

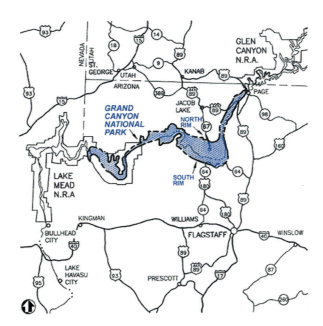

B **Analyze a Photo.** Study the picture below of the Grand Canyon taken from a satellite in space. Answer the questions in complete sentences.

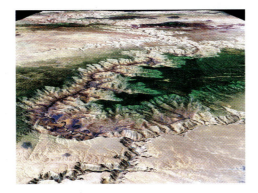

1. What can you observe about the Grand Canyon's shape?

2. What colors do you see? What do you think the colors show?

3. How does this picture help you learn more about the Grand Canyon?

4. What new questions do you have about the Grand Canyon?

READING

 A **Read.** Read this geography textbook article about the Grand Canyon.

The Grand Canyon

The Grand Canyon is one of Earth's most amazing places. Tourists, scientists, and environmentalists from all over the world treasure the canyon. The Grand Canyon is important because of its size, formation, and beauty.

The Size of the Grand Canyon

Located in the southwest United States, the Grand Canyon is the longest canyon in the world. It stretches 277 miles from the beginning of the Paria River in Arizona to the Grand Wash Cliffs near the Nevada border. At its widest point, it is eighteen miles across. At its deepest point, it is nearly six thousand feet, or one mile, down. The Grand Canyon looks like a giant piece of the Earth that was sliced out. One might imagine that a sudden, violent force caused such an enormous break in the Earth. Yet the canyon was formed over millions of years by slow but powerful forces.

The Formation of the Grand Canyon

The Grand Canyon was mainly carved by the Colorado River. This river runs along the bottom of the canyon. Millions of years ago, the Colorado River ran along the Earth's surface. The river slowly eroded, or wore away, the rocks over a very long period of time. The Grand Canyon was formed where two plates, or sections, of the Earth's surface join together. When these plates slowly moved together, land on one side of the river pushed upward. This upward movement made it easier for the river to erode, or carve, the huge canyon. In addition to its size and interesting formation, the Grand Canyon's beauty makes it one of the most popular places to visit in the world.

The Grand Canyon's Beauty

The colors of the Grand Canyon give it incredible beauty. The land surrounding the canyon is dry, rocky, and dotted with tall, flat-topped hills, called buttes. Thick, coarse plants, like sagebrush and cactus, grow at the top of the buttes. They splash the tan countryside with green. Nearer to the canyon, the land and rocks grow redder. Then the walls of the canyon show layers of ancient rock laid on top of each other. Like a sunset, some areas of color are thick and others are thin. Near the top, or the rim, the colors of the rock layers are lighter—tan, brown, and gray. In the walls near the bottom of the canyon, the colors deepen from yellow, red, and orange, to brown, almost black, and violet. With so many different colors, it is no wonder that millions of people visit the Grand Canyon each year. This year will be the same. Scientists, tourists, and environmentalists all will come to enjoy and study the canyon's enormous size and beauty.

Sources:
Fraser, Mary Ann. In Search of the Grand Canyon: Down the Colorado with John Wesley Powell. New York: Henry Holt and Co., Inc., 1995.
Mahanay, Mike. "Geology and Geography of the Grand Canyon." Grand Canyon Treks. 1997-2002. 8 Dec. 2007 <http://www.grandcanyontreks.org/geology.htm>.
Vieira, Linda. Grand Canyon: A Trail through Time. New York: Walker and Company, 1997.

VOCABULARY

A Find each word in the reading on page 4. Look at the words around it to guess the meaning. Compare your answers with a partner.

Nouns	Verbs	Adjectives	
~~geography~~	carve	ancient	giant
force	slice	coarse	redder
formation	splash	enormous	rocky
layer	stretch	flat-topped	violent

B Complete the sentences about the Grand Canyon. Use the correct form of the words in the box.

1. The _____*geography*_____ textbook article describes the Grand Canyon's size and beauty.

2. There is also an interesting paragraph on the _____ of the Grand Canyon in which the author describes how the canyon was formed.

3. The Grand Canyon is the longest canyon in the world. You would think that a _____ event formed it.

4. The canyon actually was _____ by a river over millions of years.

5. It's amazing that a river could _____ through such hard, _____ ground.

6. _____ of colorful, very old rock form the walls of the canyon.

C Answer these questions using the words from the box.

1. What is the study of the earth's surface? _____*geography*_____

2. What two words mean *big*? _____ _____

3. What is the power to do something? _____

4. What can you do with water? _____

5. What word means to go off for a long way? _____

6. What two words refer to cutting away something? _____ _____

7. What word means *very old*? _____

8. What word means more and more red? _____

GRAMMAR ➤ Learn more in the Grammar Reference, pages 172-179.

Simple Regular Tenses		
Regular Past	**Regular Present**	**Regular Future**
Millions of people **visited** the Grand Canyon last year.	Millions of people **visit** the Grand Canyon this year.	Millions of people **will visit** the Grand Canyon next year.

Some common verbs are irregular in the past and present:

be	was, were	am, is, are
go	went	go, goes
have	had	has, have

A Complete the chart with sentences from the reading on page 4.

Regular Past	1.	When these plates slowly moved together, land on one side of the river pushed upward.
	2.	
Regular Present	3.	
	4.	
Regular Future	5.	
	6.	
Irregular Past	7.	
	8.	
Irregular Present	9.	
	10.	

Prepositional Phrases for Location		
Sentence	**Noun**	**Prepositional Phrase**
Near the top of the canyon, the colors are lighter.	top	near the top of the canyon
In the walls, the colors deepen.	walls	in the walls

In a sentence, **prepositions** show the relationship between a noun and something else in the sentence. Often, prepositions tell where something is located or where something takes place. **Prepositional phrases** are made up of the preposition, the noun to which it is related, and any adjectives of that noun.

B Complete the sentences with prepositions from the box. Then underline the prepositional phrases.

| below | to | in between | ~~from~~ | across from | along | in |

1. People _____ *from* _____ all parts of the world visit the Grand Canyon.
2. The canyon is _____ the southwest region of the United States.
3. It is more than two hundred miles from one end of the canyon _____ the other.
4. One edge of the canyon is eighteen miles _____ the other.
5. Today, the Colorado River runs _____ the canyon walls, _____ the Earth's surface.
6. Millions of years ago, the river ran _____ the Earth's surface.

ORGANIZATION

Three-Paragraph Essay

Re-read the article on page 4. Complete the outline with information from the article.

Remember!
A three-paragraph essay begins with an **introduction paragraph** that gives general, important information about the topic. This paragraph ends with a **thesis statement**, a sentence that summarizes the main ideas of the essay. The **body paragraph** begins with a **topic sentence**, includes major and minor **supporting sentences**, and ends with a **concluding sentence**. The **concluding paragraph** summarizes and ends the essay.

The Grand Canyon

I. Introduction
 A. Amazing
 B. Tourists, scientists, and environmentalists treasure it
 C. Thesis Statement: **1.** *The Grand Canyon is important because of its size, formation, and beauty.*

II. Body
 A. Size of the Grand Canyon: Topic sentence: **2.** _____
  a. Major supporting sentence: **3.** *It stretches 277 miles from the beginning of the Paria River in Arizona to the Grand Wash Cliffs near the Nevada border.*
  b. Minor supporting sentence: width: **4.** _____
  c. Minor supporting sentence: height: **5.** _____
  d. Concluding sentence: **6.** _____
 B. Formation of the Grand Canyon: Topic sentence: **7.** _____
  a. Major supporting sentence: **8.** _____
  b. Minor supporting sentence: **9.** _____
  c. Minor supporting sentence: plate movement: **10.** _____
  d. Concluding sentence: **11.** _____

III. Conclusion

    A. Topic sentence: **12.** *The colors of the Grand Canyon give it incredible beauty.*

        a. Major supporting sentence: **13.** _____

        b. Minor supporting sentence: **14.** _____

Spatial Order

Begin at the top of this diagram of the Grand Canyon and work down. Label each part of the Grand Canyon according to the information in the reading on page 4.

> **Remember!**
> Essays about places are often organized by **spatial order**. Spatial order gives information by location, or the way the author sees places.

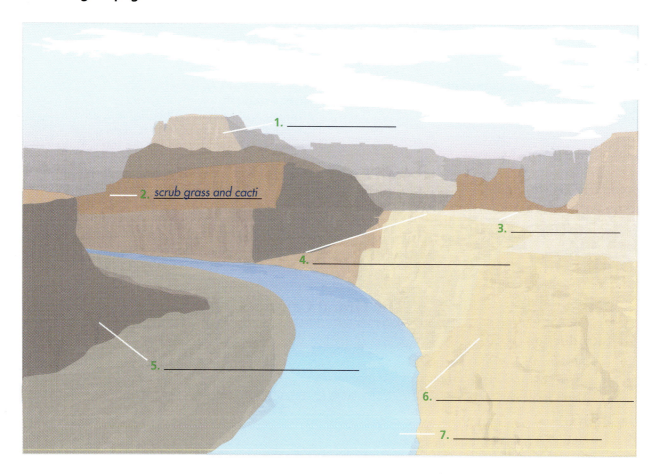

1. _____

2. *scrub grass and cacti*

3. _____

4. _____

5. _____

6. _____

7. _____

WRITING STRATEGIES

Remember!
Vivid description uses sensory adjectives that appeal to all five senses. Also, vivid descriptive writing includes strong verbs that show exactly what the author means.

Vivid Description

A Write sentences about the Grand Canyon using the adjectives and verbs from the box. Use each word only once.

~~ancient~~   coarse   enormous   rocky   violent   carve   slice   splash

Tell about the age of the canyon.

1. *The Grand Canyon is an ancient rock formation.*

Tell about the size of the canyon.

2. _____

Tell about the formation of the canyon.

3. _____

4. _____

5. _____

Tell about the land around the canyon.

6. _____

7. _____

8. _____

B Close your eyes and imagine each place or scene listed below. What do you see? What do you hear? What do you smell? What do you feel? List at least three descriptive words for each place or scene. Use your dictionary to look up words if needed.

1. the Grand Canyon
   enormous, rough, windy

2. a mountain lake at sunrise
   _____

3. a rainforest full of wild animals
   _____

4. an erupting volcano
   _____

5. a big city at rush hour

_____

6. a crowded sports stadium

_____

7. your school's cafeteria during lunchtime

_____

8. your school's library

_____

WRITING CONVENTIONS

Commas with Prepositional Phrases

Add a comma or commas to each sentence.

1. When we went to visit the Grand Canyon, we flew into Phoenix, Arizona.

2. First we flew over the canyon in a helicopter and then we hiked down the canyon on mules.

3. From the sky we saw rough land that surrounds the canyon.

4. As I looked out the window I saw the many colors of the canyon walls.

5. White red tan and orange layers make the canyon look like the sun painted them with its own rays.

6. My mother father brother and I rode mules to the bottom of the canyon.

7. I was nervous and uncomfortable on the mule's back but what I saw around me was worth my troubles.

8. For our next vacation we will visit Chicago Illinois.

> **Remember!**
> Use a **comma (,)** to help a reader separate the parts of a sentence.
> - a city from a state: Winslow, Arizona
> - a series of three or more items: size, formation, and beauty
> - two sentences that are joined with **and, but,** or **or**: The Grand Canyon is the longest canyon in the world, but it is not the deepest.
> - after a phrase that begins a sentence: Nearer to the canyon, the land and rocks grow redder.

Expository Writing

Expository writing explains a topic. A **descriptive** essay describes a person, place, or thing in such detail that the reader can picture and understand it. Also, the description often explains why that person, place, or thing is important. A geography textbook, a travel magazine article, and a descriptive essay contain examples of descriptive writing.

 A **Read.** Read Sandra's descriptive essay.

The Alamo

by Sandra Sanchez

Although I have lived in Texas all my life, I never saw the Alamo before last summer. The Alamo became important to me only after I learned why it was important to others.

This year in school, we studied the battle of the Alamo. I learned that before the 1850s, the southwestern United States was part of Mexico. The ruler of Mexico, General Santa Anna, wouldn't let the people of Mexico govern themselves. Many people living in Texas became angry. They declared their independence from Mexico. Santa Anna marched with thousands of troops to fight these Texas rebels. When they arrived in San Antonio, about 200 men and some women and children hid in a fort called the Alamo. Some were Mexicans who had lived in San Antonio for generations. Some were people from the United States who had come to Texas for cheap land and a new life. Santa Anna's troops surrounded the little fort. At dawn, they attacked. The battle was short but violent. The two hundred people inside the Alamo held the fort for only two hours. Yet they killed five hundred of Santa Anna's soldiers. When the battle was over, all but two of the men in the Alamo were dead. Then people all over the United States heard about their bravery and Santa Anna's cruelty. People went to Texas to help Texans fight for their independence. The brave people of the Alamo inspired other Americans to fight for Texans' freedom.

After studying the history of the Alamo, I went with my family to see it. When we arrived, I felt disappointed at first. All that remains of the Alamo is the church where the women and children hid during the battle. I had hoped to see the whole fort. However, when I walked through the doors, I forgot my disappointment. It was cool and dark inside. I blinked to let my eyes adjust. As I walked down the middle of the church, I breathed deeply. I smelled the chalky, limestone walls and the dusty, ancient wooden beams. I stopped and listened to the quiet shuffle of the other visitors' footsteps. I imagined what the women and children must have heard during the battle as they crouched in the darkness. Like me they were Mexican, American, and Texan. Like me they wanted to be free. My heart beat faster as I remembered the people who had lost their lives to make Texas free. I know now I will always remember the Alamo.

Sources:
Garland, Sherry. <u>Voices of the Alamo</u>. New York: Scholastic Press, 2000.
Tanaka, Shelley. <u>A Day that Changed America: The Alamo</u>. New York: Hyperion Books for Children, 2003.

STEP-BY-STEP WRITING

Purpose: Describe an Interesting Place

WRITING PROMPT

Think of a place that you want to describe. It must be a place that has meaning to you and to other people who go there. Write a three-paragraph expository descriptive essay describing the place so that your classmates can picture it and understand its importance.

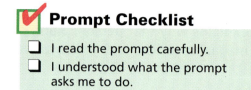

Prompt Checklist

- [ ] I read the prompt carefully.
- [ ] I understood what the prompt asks me to do.

STEP 1 Pre-write

A Look at Sandra's diagram. Make your own sketch or diagram of your place. If needed, research about the place and make notes on your sketch.

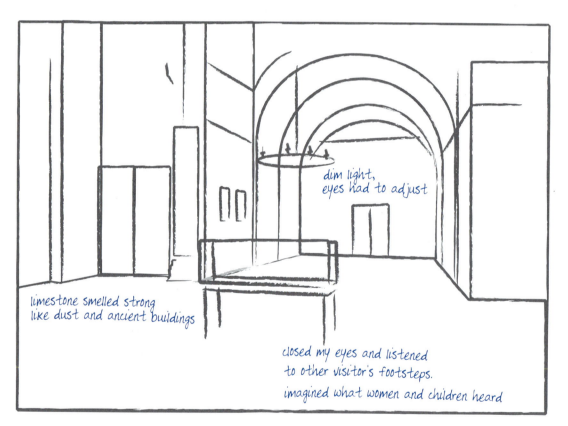

dim light, eyes had to adjust

limestone smelled strong like dust and ancient buildings

closed my eyes and listened to other visitor's footsteps.
imagined what women and children heard

B Close your eyes and imagine you are at your place. Make a list of adjectives to describe the place.

cool	chalky
dark	dusty
	quiet

STEP 2 Organize

Look at Sandra's essay outline. Create your own essay outline with information that you will include in your essay.

Sandra's Essay Outline

The Alamo

I. **Introduction**

A. I have lived in Texas my whole life.

B. I had not seen the Alamo.

C. Thesis Statement: The Alamo became important to me only after I learned why it was important to others.

II. **Body**

A. Battle of the Alamo: Topic sentence: This year in school, we studied the battle of the Alamo.

   a. Major supporting sentence: We learned that before the 1850s, the southwestern United States was part of Mexico.

   b. Minor supporting sentence: The ruler of Mexico, General Santa Anna, wouldn't let the people of Mexico govern themselves.

   c. Minor supporting sentence: When the battle was over, all but two of the men in the Alamo were dead.

   d. Concluding sentence: The brave people of the Alamo inspired other Americans to fight for Texans' freedom.

III. **Conclusion**

A. Topic sentence: After studying the history of the Alamo, I went with my family to see it.

   a. at first: disappointed

   b. interior: cool, dark, quiet, dusty, chalky

   c. Concluding sentence: I know now I will always remember the Alamo.

STEP 3 Draft and Revise

A **Practice.** Look at Sandra's first draft. How can she improve it? Answer the questions on page 15.

First Draft

The Alamo

by Sandra Sanchez

(1) Although I have lived in Texas all my life, I never saw the Alamo before last summer. (2) The Alamo became important to me only after I learned why it was important to others.

(3) This year in school, we studied the battle of the Alamo. (4) I learned that before the 1850s, the southwestern United States was part of Mexico. (5) The ruler of Mexico, General Santa Anna, wouldn't let the people of Mexico govern themselves. (6) Many people living in Texas became angry. (7) They declared their independence from Mexico. (8) Santa Anna marched with thousands of troops to fight these Texas rebels. (9) When they arrived in San Antonio, about 200 men and some women and children hid in a fort called the Alamo. (10) Some were Mexicans who had lived in San Antonio for generations. (11) Some were people from the United States who had come to Texas for cheap land and a new life. (12) Santa Anna's troops surrounded the little fort. (13) At dawn, they attacked. (14) The battle was short but violent. (15) The two hundred people held the fort for only two hours. (16) Yet they killed five hundred of Santa Anna's soldiers. (17) When the battle was over, all but two of the men in the Alamo were dead. (18) Then people all over the United States heard about their bravery and Santa Anna's cruelty. (19) People went to Texas to help Texans fight for their independence.

(20) After studying the history of the Alamo, I went with my family to see it. (21) When we arrived, I felt disappointed at first. (22) All that remains of the Alamo is the church where the women and children hid during the battle. (23) I had hoped to see the whole fort. (24) However, when I walked through the doors, I forgot my disappointment. (25) As I walked down the middle of the church, I breathed deeply. (26) It was cool and dark inside. (27) I blinked to let my eyes adjust. (28) I smelled the walls and the wooden beams. (29) I stopped and listened to the quiet shuffle of the other visitors' footsteps. (30) I imagined what the women and children must have heard during the battle as they sat in the darkness. (31) Like me they were Mexican American and Texan. (32) Like me, they wanted to be free. (33) My heart beat faster as I remembered the people who had lost their lives to make Texas free. (34) I know now I will always remember the Alamo.

1. What prepositional phrase can Sandra add to sentence 15 after the phrase *The 200 people* to make the sentence clearer?

   A fighting

   B in San Antonio

   C inside the Alamo

   D near the soldiers

2. How can Sandra BEST conclude paragraph 2?

   A That's what I learned about the Alamo.

   B There were also common people like eight-year-old Enrique Esparza hiding in the fort.

   C The brave people of the Alamo inspired other Americans to fight for Texans' freedom.

   D You should also visit the Alamo if you ever get the chance.

3. Which sentence seems out of spatial order?

   A sentence 24

   B sentence 25

   C sentence 26

   D sentence 27

4. How can Sandra add sensory adjectives to sentence 28 to make the writing more vivid?

   A I smelled the chalky, limestone walls and the dusty, ancient wooden beams.

   B I smelled the big walls and the long wooden beams.

   C I breathed in the walls and the wooden beams.

   D I smelled the hard walls and the rough wooden beams.

5. How can Sandra change the verb *sat* in sentence 30 to make the writing more vivid?

   A change *sat* to *sit*

   B change *sat* to *will sit*

   C change *sat* to *stood*

   D change *sat* to *crouched*

6. Where should Sandra add commas in sentence 31?

   A Like me they were Mexican, American, and Texan.

   B Like me, they were Mexican, American, and Texan.

   C Like me, they were Mexican American, and Texan.

   D Like me, they were Mexican American and Texan.

B **Draft.** Write a first draft of your expository descriptive essay. Use your notes from Steps 1 and 2.

C **Revise.** Read your first draft. How can you improve it? Look at the revision checklist. Revise your writing.

✔ **Revision Checklist**

❏ I described the place using sensory adjectives and specific verbs.

❏ I explained the importance of the place.

❏ I organized my essay with a thesis statement, topic sentences, major and minor supporting sentence, and a concluding sentence.

❏ I used spatial order to organize my description.

STEP 4 Edit

A **Practice.** Look at the sentences. Choose the best word or phrase to complete each sentence.

1. The Vietnam War Memorial _____ important to me and many other people.
   A am
   Ⓑ is
   C are
   D were

2. Located _____ Washington D.C., the memorial honors all the United States soldiers who died during the Vietnam War.
   A on
   B to
   C for
   D in

3. Maya Lin _____ the memorial when she was only 21 years old.
   A design
   B designs
   C designed
   D will design

4. _____ the memorial was completed.
   A In 1982
   B In 1982,
   C At 1982
   D At 1982,

5. The memorial is _____ wall of black stone in a giant v-shape with the names of thousands of soldiers carved on it.
   A an enormous
   B a violent
   C a redder
   D an ancient

6. Currently, 58,249 names are carved on it, _____ this number can change.
   A although
   B for
   C to
   D until

7. Even though I live _____, I want to go to the Vietnam War Memorial.
   A to Sacramento California
   B to Sacramento, California
   C in Sacramento, California
   D in Sacramento California

8. I _____ the memorial in Washington, D.C. next year.
   A visit
   B visits
   C visited
   D will visit

B **Edit.** Re-read your draft from Step 3. Look at the editing checklist. Edit your writing.

 C **Peer Edit.** Exchange drafts with a partner. Tell your partner what you like about the draft. Look at the editing checklist. Tell your partner how to improve the draft.

✔ Editing Checklist

me	my partner	
☐	☐	used simple regular and irregular past, present, and future verbs correctly
☐	☐	used prepositional phrases correctly
☐	☐	used correct spelling, capitalization, and punctuation (especially commas) correctly

STEP 5 Publish

Write your expository descriptive essay in your best handwriting or use a computer. Look at Sandra's essay on page 11 for ideas. Remember to include a title and your name. Add a photograph or drawing to your essay if you want. Present your essay to the class.

TECHNOLOGY

Finding Photographs and Maps Online to Create an Information Sheet

- Go to an Internet search engine. Select the "images" search button.
- Type in the place you described in your essay.
- Find a photograph or map that is interesting and appropriate for your descriptive essay.
- Create an information sheet for your classmates with a publishing program.
- Use and cite the Web site.

Unit 2

Describe a Person You Admire

UNIT OBJECTIVES

Writing
biographical narrative

Organization
chronological order
timelines

Writing Strategies
inferring meaning
time-order words as transitions

Writing Conventions
reported speech

Vocabulary
personality adjectives

Grammar
simple past tense with action
   verbs
simple past vs. past continuous
   tense
compound sentences with
   conjunctions

Technology
finding and citing online sources

George Washington Carver

A **Analyze a Photo.** Look at the photos of George Washington Carver on this page and on page 18. Answer the questions with a partner.

1. What do you already know about George Washington Carver?

2. What questions do you have about George Washington Carver?

3. Describe the photos. Does the information in the photos answer any of your questions?

4. What questions do you still have about George Washington Carver?

 B **Analyze a Chart.** Look at the chart below. Answer the following questions with a partner.

1. What does this chart show?

2. About how many food uses and recipes did George Washington Carver develop?

3. About how many non-food uses did he develop?

4. Do you eat or use any of these products? Which ones?

5. What does this chart tell you about George Washington Carver?

Some By-Products and Recipes from Peanuts by George Washington Carver

FOOD PRODUCTS

bar candy	cocoa	meat substitutes
buttermilk	cooking oil	peanut brittle, butter, and cake
caramel	cream candy	peanut flour
chili sauce	instant coffee	vinegar
chocolate-covered peanuts	mayonnaise	peanut foods for animals

NON-FOOD PRODUCTS

Cosmetics	laundry soap	axle grease
all-purpose cream	peanut oil shampoo	charcoal from shells
antiseptic soap	shaving cream	glue
baby massage cream		insulating boards
face cream and powder	**Household**	printer's ink
hand lotion	dyes, paints, and stains	wood filler
oil for hair and scalp	medicines	

A **Read.** Read the biographical narrative about George Washington Carver.

George Washington Carver

George Washington Carver was an admirable scientist and humanitarian who changed farming in the United States forever. In 1864, near the end of the American Civil War, he was born on a farm in Missouri. His parents were slaves on the farm. After the Civil War ended, the farm owner, Moses Carver, and his wife raised George as their own child. George grew up knowing and loving farm plants.

Education was Carver's greatest aspiration and challenge throughout his childhood. He once said that education was the key to unlock the golden door of freedom. Carver had to move away from home to attend school. He made this sacrifice and many others to finish grade school and high school. Later he became the first African-American to attend Simpson College and the first African-American professor to teach at Iowa College. Because of his struggles to gain an education, Carver said that there is no shortcut to achievement.

Carver was an agricultural scientist, or a scientist who studies farming. He discovered hundreds of uses for crops like peanuts, soybeans, and sweet potatoes. At Tuskegee Institute, Carver was head of the agricultural department from 1897 until his death in 1943. He taught a new way of farming called crop rotation. For years, farmers living in the southern United States had grown tobacco and cotton. These two crops take important nutrients out of the soil so that each year it is harder to grow the crops. Carver taught southern farmers to rotate, or go back and forth, between cotton and tobacco crops and other crops that bring back the nutrients in the soil. Carver's crop rotation way of farming forever changed and saved southern farming. Carver also developed numerous industrial uses from farming. He discovered or improved glues, chili sauce, paper, plastic, wood stain, and many, many more products. Carver's contributions to farming and the world seem countless.

One might expect that such an intelligent, influential, and successful man would be proud and selfish, yet Carver was humble and generous. Although he invented many farming industrial developments, he didn't sell his ideas to make money. Instead, he gave his ideas to the whole country freely. He said that God gave him the ideas, so how could he sell them? When offered a salary of $100,000 per year (equal to about a million dollars today), he declined. Instead, he chose to continue to teach at Tuskegee and to help farmers. At the end of his life, Carver donated all of the money he had saved during his life to Tuskegee Institute for students to continue their research, or studies, in agriculture. The writing on his gravestone describes Carver best as a man who could have added fortune to fame, but caring for neither, found happiness and honor in being helpful to the world. George Washington Carver is one of the United States's most admirable people for his contributions to agriculture and for his kindness.

Source:
Adler, David A. George Washington Carver. New York: Holiday House, 1999.

VOCABULARY

A Find each word in the reading on page 20. Look at the words around it to guess the meaning. Compare your answers with a partner.

Nouns	Verbs	Adjectives	
achievement	honor	admirable	proud
aspiration	humanitarian	generous	selfish
challenge	sacrifice	humble	successful
contribution	donate	influential	
	invent	intelligent	

B Match the word with its definition. Write the definitions next to the words.

1. admirable ___c. worthy of being thought well of___

2. intelligent _____

3. selfish _____

4. humble _____

5. generous _____

6. humanitarian _____

7. aspiration _____

8. sacrifice _____

9. achievement _____

10. contribution _____

a. a person who is concerned about the well-being of all people

b. only thinking of oneself

c. ~~worthy of being thought well of~~

d. a gift of time, talent, or money

e. giving freely and a lot

f. a goal or desire

g. an accomplishment or success

h. smart, bright

i. a giving up of something of value for someone else

j. modest; not thinking yourself greater than others

C Answer these questions using the vocabulary words from the box in activity A.

1. What are we doing when we create something that has never been created before?

2. What do we call people who make a difference in others' lives?

3. What do we call people who have fame, fortune, or the ability to achieve what they want?

4. What are we doing when we give something away freely?

5. What do we call people who think very well of themselves?

6. What word do we use to describe people whom we respect?

7. What do we often call a difficult situation?

8. Which word means *a strong desire to achieve something important?*

Unit 2 Describe a Person You Admire **21**

Simple Past Tense with Action Verbs

Verb	Sentence with Past Tense Form
change	George Washington Carver **changed** farm practices in the United States forever.
give	Carver **gave** his ideas to the whole country freely.

To form the past tense with regular verbs, you add *-ed: change* becomes *changed.*
To form the past tense with irregular verbs, you change the spelling: *give* becomes *gave.*
For a list of irregular verbs and their past tense forms, see the grammar reference on pages 172-179.

A Complete the sentences with the past tense form of the verbs in the box. Use each verb only once.

| play | ~~raise~~ | move | grow | build | want |

1. Moses Carver and his wife _____*raised*_____ George as their own child.

2. As a boy, George _____ his own garden where he learned about plants.

3. Because it was difficult and even dangerous for African Americans to go to school at that time, Carver _____ many times to find safe and high-quality schools.

4. When he was first rejected from college because of his race, Carver bought farmland and _____ his own house out of mud.

5. Still, Carver _____ to study and learn. So he tried again to get into college.

6. At college, Carver studied hard, but he also _____ football and joined many clubs.

Past Continuous Tense

Verb	Sentence with Past Continuous Form
end	George was born in the South when the Civil War **was ending**.
become	Slaves, like George's parents, **were becoming** free.

To form the past continuous, use *was* or *were* and the *-ing* form of the verb.
The simple past and past continuous tenses often show the relationship between two different actions. The past continuous is used to describe an action that was going on when another action took place and ended.

B Complete the sentences. Use the simple past or past continuous forms of the verbs in parentheses.

1. Carver _____tried_____ (try) to get an education at a time when few African Americans _____going_____ (go) to school.

2. Carver _____ (study) agriculture because he _____ (plan) to help Southern farmers, especially African Americans, when he graduated.

3. Through his studies, Carver _____ (discover) that the South's two biggest crops, cotton and tobacco, _____ (ruin) the soil.

4. Carver _____ (find) that as peanuts and sweet potatoes grew, they fed the soil.

5. Carver _____ (write) instructions for farmers to grow peanuts and sweet potatoes.

6. Carver _____ (is) pleased to see that farmers _____ (learn) to plant new crops because of his teachings.

Compound Sentences with Conjunctions	
Two Simple Sentences	**Compound Sentence**
One might imagine that such an intelligent, influential, and successful man would be proud and selfish. Yet Carver was humble and generous.	One might imagine that such an intelligent, influential, and successful man would be proud and selfish, yet Carver was humble and generous.

A **conjunction** is a word like *and, so,* or *but.* Conjunctions can join two sentences. This joined sentence is called a compound sentence. Use a comma between the two sentences.

C Rewrite the pairs of simple sentences to change them into compound sentences. Use the conjunctions in parentheses.

1. Tuskegee Institute was established in 1881 to train African-Americans for work. Carver became head of its department of agriculture in 1896. (and)

   Tuskegee Institute was established in 1881 to train African-Americans for work, and Carver became

   head of its department of agriculture in 1896.

2. Constantly planting crops like cotton ruined the soil. In some years, beetles destroyed entire crops. (and)

   _____

   _____

3. Carver knew southern farming had to be changed. It might be destroyed forever. (or)

   _____

   _____

4. Carver knew that people could not eat as many peanuts and sweet potatoes as Southern farmers would grow. He looked for new uses for these vegetables. (so)

_____

_____

5. Thomas Edison offered Carver a large salary to work for him. Carver declined. (but)

_____

_____

6. In 1923, Carver won the Spingarn Medal. In 1939, he was given the Theodore Roosevelt Medal. (and)

_____

_____

ORGANIZATION

Remember!
Biographies are usually organized in **chronological order**. This means that the **sequence of events** is ordered by time. However, time is not the most important information. The subject, George Washington Carver, is more important. Time only provides a frame for telling about the subject.

Chronological Order

Complete the outline with information from the reading on page 20.

George Washington Carver

I. **Background: George's childhood**
   A. When? 1. _He was born in 1864 on a Missouri farm._
   B. Who? 2. _____
   C. What did he learn from his childhood? 3. _____
II. **Background: Carver's schooling**
   A. Why? 4. _____
   B. Where? 5. _____
   C. What was significant about Carver's schooling? 6. _____
III. **Contributions to agriculture**
   A. What did he study? 7. _____
   B. Why? 8. _____
   C. How did his science affect the world? 9. _____
IV. **Carver as a humanitarian**
   A. What was he like? 10. _____
   B. How do we know this? 11. _____
   C. For what is Carver remembered? 12. _____

Timelines

Complete the timeline with dates and events from the reading on page 20.

from the reading on page 20.

1. _1864_   3. _____   5. _____

2. _GW Carver born._   4. _____   6. _____

WRITING STRATEGIES

Inferring Meaning

Reread the biographical narrative on page 20.
With a partner or small group, discuss the following questions. You will need to make inferences, or guesses, based on the information in the reading and your own knowledge.

1. Why did George Washington Carver make so many sacrifices to get an education?

2. What did Carver mean when he said there is no short cut to achievement?

3. Why didn't Carver sell most of his discoveries?

4. What does the quote on Carver's gravestone mean? How does it apply to Carver's life?

Time-Order Words

Re-read the biographical narrative on page 20. In the chart, write the sentences that use the time-order words. Then identify the ideas that are being connected with the transition word.

Remember!

Use time-order words to make smooth transitions or connections from sentence to sentence and paragraph to paragraph. Some common time-order words are: *after, before, during, until, soon, later, finally, then, next, when.*

Time-Order Word	Sentence from the Reading	Ideas Being Connected
After	1. After the Civil War ended, the farm owner, Moses Carver, and his wife raised George as their own child.	George's childhood and the Civil War
During	2. _____	_____
Later	3. _____	_____
Until	4. _____	_____
When	5. _____	_____

WRITING CONVENTIONS

Remember!

Reported speech tells what someone said without quoting him or her directly. Reported speech does not use quotation marks. Usually reported speech uses some form of the phrase *He said that*. No comma is needed to indicate reported speech.

Reported Speech

Re-read the biographical narrative on page 20. Find the reported speech sentences that contain the direct speech quotes below. Write the reported speech sentences on the lines.

1. He once said, "Education is the key to unlock the golden door of freedom."

   _____

2. Carver said, "There is no short cut to achievement."

   _____

3. He said, "God gave them to me. How could I sell them to someone else?"

   _____

Biographical Narrative

A **biographical narrative** is a true story about someone's life, written by another person. A biography lists important **dates**, **events**, and **people** in the person's life. A biography usually begins with the person's birth and ends with his or her death. If the person is still alive, a biography ends with what he or she is doing now.

 A **Read.** Read Jaime's biographical narrative of Cesar Chavez.

Cesar Chavez

by Jaime Garcia

I admire Cesar Chavez for his dedication to making a better world, no matter the cost to himself. As a farmer and activist, Chavez spent his life fighting for farmers' rights. Born in 1927 on his family's farm in Arizona, Chavez grew up as a farmer. During the Great Depression, his father could not afford to run the family farm, so they became migrant workers. This meant that throughout Chavez's childhood, his family lived a few months at a time on farms throughout the southwestern United States. After completing the eighth grade, Chavez left school to work on the farms to help support his family. It was a hard life. The family worked hard for little pay and no health care.

In 1952, Cesar Chavez began his work as an activist, fighting for others' rights. While gathering crops at an apricot farm, Chavez met Fred Ross, an organizer of the Community Service Organization (CSO), which helped people with immigration problems. Within a few months, Cesar Chavez was working full-time for CSO. He helped Mexican Americans like himself by fighting racism, registering them to vote, and helping them start new CSO chapters throughout California. By the 1960s, Chavez was acting as the national director of CSO, but he hadn't forgotten the migrant workers in the fields. He tried to convince CSO to support the farm workers. When CSO would not help, Chavez gave up his job and founded the National Farm Workers Association (NFWA). This was a difficult time for Chavez and his family. His wife had to work in the fields all day while Chavez worked hard to organize the farm workers so that they could gain more rights, such as better pay and health care for their families. Chavez said that because he was outraged at the farm workers' conditions, he couldn't be free or happy until he had worked to change them. Chavez spent all of his life until his death in 1993 fasting, lobbying, and fighting for migrant workers' rights.

Cesar Chavez is my hero because he sacrificed and fought hard for others' rights. I am Mexican American. After I go to college, I will come back to my community and follow Chavez's example. I will work hard to help others in need gain the rights they deserve.

Sources:
Cesar Chavez. University of California. 14 May 2007 <http://clnet.ucla.edu/research/chavez/bio/>.
Soto, Gary. Cesar Chavez: A Hero for Everyone. New York: Aladdin Paperbacks, 2003.

STEP-BY-STEP WRITING

Purpose: Describe a Person You Admire

WRITING PROMPT

Think of a famous person you admire. Research the person's life in at least two sources. (See Technology on page 33 for information about finding and citing sources.) Write a three-paragraph biographical narrative about the person's important dates, events, and contributions. Be sure to explain to your teacher, classmates, and possible newspaper audience why you admire the person.

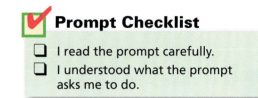

Prompt Checklist

☐ I read the prompt carefully.
☐ I understood what the prompt asks me to do.

STEP 1 Pre-write

Look at Jaime's list about Cesar Chavez. Make your own list of words and phrases that describe the person you admire. Don't stop until you run out of ideas. Does your list include **who, what, when, where, why,** and **how**? From your list, circle the words and ideas you want to include in your composition.

Jaime's List

inspiring	soft-spoken	strikes
civil rights leader	sailor with the navy in	marches
peaceful	WWII	Mexican-American
protestor	poor	better wages
improved lives	dirty shacks	health care
migrant worker	barely survived	improved working
father	smart	conditions
8 children	whole community	win against rich and
husband	listened to him	powerful growers
shy		nonviolence

STEP 2 Organize

A Look at Jaime's outline. Make your own outline about your person.

Jaime's Outline

Title: Cesar Chavez

I. **Introduction**
   A. Why I admire Cesar Chavez
   B. Important dates and events in Chavez's childhood
   C. Connections between his childhood and later life

II. **Body**
   A. Turning point in Chavez's life
   B. Result of that turning point
   C. Chavez's contributions to the world

III. **Conclusion**
   A. Summarize Chavez's importance to the world
   B. Chavez's importance to me
   C. How I want to be like Chavez

B Look at Jaime's timeline. Use a timeline computer program or handwrite your own timeline of the important dates and events in your person's life.

Jaime's Timeline

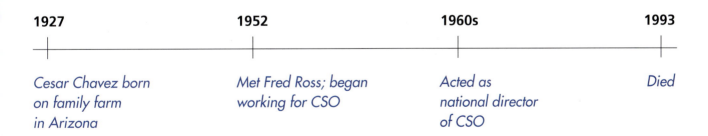

1927	1952	1960s	1993
Cesar Chavez born on family farm in Arizona	Met Fred Ross; began working for CSO	Acted as national director of CSO	Died

STEP 3 Draft and Revise

A **Practice.** Look at Jaime's first draft. How can he improve it? Answer the questions on page 31.

First Draft
Cesar Chavez
by Jaime Garcia

(1) I admire Cesar Chavez for his dedication to making a better world, no matter the cost to himself. (2) As a farmer and activist, Chavez spent his life fighting for farmers' rights. (3) During the Great Depression, his father could not afford to run the family farm so they became migrant workers. (4) This meant that throughout Chavez's childhood, his family lived a few months at a time on farms throughout the southwestern United States. (5) Born in 1927 on his family's farm in Arizona, Chavez grew up as a farmer. (6) After completing the eighth grade, Chavez left school to work on the farms to help support his family. (7) It was a hard life. (8) The family worked hard for little pay and no health care.

(8) In 1952, Cesar Chavez began his work as an activist, fighting for others' rights. (9) While gathering crops at an apricot farm, Chavez met Fred Ross, an organizer of the Community Service Organization (CSO). (10) Within a few months, Cesar Chavez worked full-time for CSO, which helped people with immigration problems. (11) He helped Mexican Americans like himself by fighting racism, registering them to vote, and helping them start new CSO chapters throughout California. (12) By the 1960s, Chavez was acting as the national director of CSO. (13) He hadn't forgotten the migrant workers in the fields. (14) He tried to convince CSO to support the farm workers. (15) CSO would not help, Chavez gave up his job and founded the National Farm Workers Association (NFWA). (16) This was a difficult time for Chavez and his family. (17) His wife had to work in the fields all day while Chavez worked hard to organize the farm workers so that they could gain more rights, such as better pay and health care for their families. (18) Chavez said, "If you're outraged at conditions, then you can't possibly be free or happy until you devote all your time to changing them and do nothing but that." (19) Chavez spent all of his life until his death in 1993 fasting, lobbying, and fighting for migrant workers' rights.

(20) Cesar Chavez is my hero because he sacrificed and fought hard for others' rights. (21) I am Mexican American. (22) After I go to college, I will come back to my community and follow Chavez's example. (23) I will work hard to help others in need gain the rights they deserve.

1. How can Jaime correct the verb *spended* in sentence 2 to be in the simple past tense?
   A change to *spend*
   B change to *was spending*
   C change to *spent*
   D change to *is going to spend*

2. Which sentence in paragraph 1 seems out of chronological order?
   A Sentence 1
   B Sentence 2
   C Sentence 5
   D Sentence 8

3. How can Jaime change the verb *worked* in sentence 10 to use the past continuous tense?
   A change to *is working*
   B change to *had working*
   C change to *will work*
   D change to *was working*

4. How can Jaime BEST combine sentences 12 and 13 to make a compound sentence?
   A By the 1960s, Chavez was acting as the national director of CSO, so he hadn't forgotten the migrant workers in the fields.
   B By the 1960s, Chavez was acting as the national director of CSO, or he hadn't forgotten the migrant workers in the fields.
   C By the 1960s, Chavez was acting as the national director of CSO, but he hadn't forgotten the migrant workers in the fields.
   D By the 1960s, Chavez was acting as the national director of CSO and he hadn't forgotten the migrant workers in the fields.

5. What time-order word can Jaime add to the beginning of sentence 15 to make a smoother transition between ideas?
   A Before
   B When
   C While
   D Soon

6. How can Jaime BEST rewrite sentence 18 to be reported speech?
   A Chavez said that because he was outraged at the farm workers' conditions, he couldn't be free or happy until he had worked to change them.
   B Chavez said, Because he was outraged at the farm workers' conditions, he couldn't be free or happy until he had worked to change them.
   C Chavez said, "that because he was outraged at the farm workers' conditions, he couldn't be free or happy until he had worked to change them."
   D Chavez said, "Because I was outraged at the farm workers' conditions, I couldn't be free or happy until I had worked to change them."

B **Draft.** Write a first draft of your biographical narrative. Use your notes from Steps 1 and 2.

C **Revise.** Read your first draft. How can you improve it? Look at the revision checklist. Revise your writing.

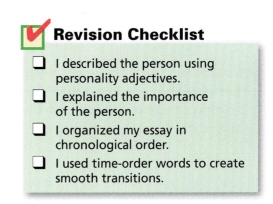
Revision Checklist
- [ ] I described the person using personality adjectives.
- [ ] I explained the importance of the person.
- [ ] I organized my essay in chronological order.
- [ ] I used time-order words to create smooth transitions.

STEP 4 Edit

A **Practice.** Look at the sentences. Choose the best substitute for the underlined words. If the sentence is correct, choose "Make no change."

1. <u>During</u> Cesar Chavez was a boy, he lived happily on his family's farm in Arizona.
   A Before
   (B) When
   C Then
   D Make no change.

2. In 1937, as the Great Depression ruined lives all across the United States, a drought <u>was destroyed</u> the Chavez's farm.
   A is destroyed
   B is destroying
   C was destroying
   D Make no change.

3. The Chavez family <u>have</u> to sell their farm and become migrant workers.
   A was having
   B had
   C is having
   D Make no change.

4. Cesar's parents tried to keep him in <u>school but after</u> eighth grade he had to drop out to begin picking crops.
   A school, but after
   B school; and after
   C school so after
   D Make no change.

5. Cesar <u>understanded</u> the suffering of the migrant worker because he lived it.
   A understood
   B understooded
   C understand
   D Make no change.

6. Cesar and his fellow migrant workers <u>were feeling</u> tired of dangerous working conditions, low pay, and no health benefits.
   A was feeling
   B is feeling
   C was felt
   D Make no change.

7. Cesar was <u>selfish</u>. He gave his time and energy freely to fight for his fellow migrant workers.
   A humble
   B generous
   C proud
   D Make no change.

8. Cesar <u>said that nonviolence</u> took more guts than violence.
   A said "nonviolence
   B said, that nonviolence
   C said, "that nonviolence
   D Make no change.

B **Edit.** Re-read your draft from Step 3. Look at the editing checklist. Edit your writing.

C **Peer Edit.** Exchange drafts with a partner. Tell your partner what you like about the draft. Look at the editing checklist. Tell your partner how to improve the draft.

✔ Editing Checklist

me	my partner	
❏	❏	used introduction, body, and conclusion paragraphs
❏	❏	used personality adjectives to describe the person
❏	❏	supported points with evidence from the person's life
❏	❏	paraphrased or quoted sources correctly
❏	❏	used simple past tense and past continuous correctly

STEP 5 Publish

Rewrite your biographical narrative in your best handwriting or use a computer. Look at Jaime's biographical narrative on page 27 for ideas. Add a photograph or drawing if you want. Present your biography to the class.

TECHNOLOGY

Finding and Citing Online Sources

- Go to an online search engine.

- Do a **keyword search** for your person. Type in the full name. Then try typing in the name and the word *quotes* to find something important your person has said.

- Select the "images" button on the search engine and find images of your person.

- Before clicking on the Web sites you found, evaluate the source. Is it reliable? The most reliable sources are encyclopedias or most museum Web sites. Can you find your person at an encyclopedia or museum site? If not, open and evaluate a *.com* or *.org* site. Does the person writing the site seem knowledgeable and unbiased?

- Find at least two reliable sources. To cite the sources for your report, use the following format:

  Web site creator's name (if given). "Web page title." <u>Web Site Title</u>. Date and/or version number. Institution or organization. Date of access <url>.

GROUP WRITING

Work in a group to write an essay about one of these topics. Follow the steps below.

1. Choose your topic.
2. Discuss and record information.
3. Do research if you need to.
4. Write a first draft.
5. Revise and edit the draft with your group.
6. Present your group's essay to the class.

Topic 1

Choose any famous person you admire. Write a three-paragraph biographical narrative about this person. Tell why you admire him or her. Tell about the important events in this person's life that have made this person who he or she is.

Rosa Parks

Roberto Clemente

Eleanor Roosevelt

Topic 2

Choose any famous place that is important to you and others. Write a three-paragraph expository essay. Tell why the place is important to you. Use your five senses to describe it so your readers can picture it in their minds.

Niagara Falls

Statue of Liberty

Hollywood, California

TIMED WRITING

Choose one writing prompt. Complete the writing task in 45 minutes.

WRITING PROMPT 1

Write a three-paragraph biographical narrative about a person in your family. Tell why this person is important to you. Tell about the important events in the family member's life so your classmates can understand this person's life.

WRITING PROMPT 2

Choose a place that is special to you. Write a three-paragraph expository essay. Tell why the place is important to only you. Use your five senses to describe it so your classmates can picture it in their minds.

Test Tip

Organize! Use graphic organizers like outlines and timelines to organize your writing. Remember to write a thesis statement for your essay. Write a topic sentence for each paragraph.

SELF-CHECK

Think about your writing skills. Check (✔) the answers that are true.

1. I understand . . .
   - ❏ sensory adjectives.
   - ❏ personality adjectives.
   - ❏ words that convey meaning.

2. I can correctly. . .
   - ❏ use sensory adjectives.
   - ❏ use strong, specific verbs.
   - ❏ infer meanings from a reading.
   - ❏ use time-transition words.

3. I can correctly use . . .
   - ❏ simple, regular and irregular past, present, and future tenses.
   - ❏ prepositional phrases for location.
   - ❏ simple past tense with action verbs.
   - ❏ past continuous tense.
   - ❏ compound sentences with conjunctions.

4. I can correctly use . . .
   - ❏ commas.
   - ❏ reported speech.

5. I can organize my writing . . .
   - ❏ in three-paragraph essays.
   - ❏ by spatial order.
   - ❏ by chronological order.
   - ❏ with a timeline.

7. I can write to . . .
   - ❏ describe.
   - ❏ narrate.

Unit 3

Write a Letter of Complaint

UNIT OBJECTIVES

Writing
business letter of complaint

Organization
order of importance

Writing Strategies
register
compare and contrast

Writing Conventions
business letter forms

Vocabulary
complaint words

Grammar
present tense and present
  continuous tense
sentences with adjective clauses

Technology
finding consumer protection
  resources online

PRE-READING

 A **Interpret an Image.** Look at the image on page 36. Answer the questions with a partner.

1. What is the image called? What does it show?

2. Name some of the foods that you see along the bottom of the pyramid.

3. What are the names of the categories for these foods?

4. Why do you think some of the categories of the pyramid are wider than others?

5. Do you eat some foods from each category at each meal? Why or why not?

East Side High School Lunch Menu

October

Monday	Tuesday	Wednesday	Thursday	Friday
1	2 MILK IS INCLUDED WITH ALL MEALS 1%, Skim, Low Fat Chocolate or Strawberry	3 No School	4 HOT DOG IN A ROLL PEANUT BUTTER/JELLY SANDWICH FRIES FRESH OR CANNED FRUIT	5 Pizza TOSSED SALAD TUNA SALAD SUB TOMATO SOUP FRESH OR CANNED FRUIT
6 CHICKEN FINGERS FRIES EGG SALAD SUB CARROTS FRESH OR CANNED FRUIT	7 BBQ RIB ON A ROLL TURKEY & CHEESE SUB RICE GREEN BEANS FRESH OR CANNED FRUIT	8 PASTA WITH SAUCE HAM & CHEESE SUB TOSSED SALAD FRESH OR CANNED FRUIT	9 BACON BURGER with CHEESE ON ROLL FRIES TURKEY & CHEESE SUB VEGETABLE STICKS FRESH OR CANNED FRUIT	10 CHICKEN FAJITAS BROWN RICE CORN TUNA SALAD SUB VEGETABLE STICKS FRESH OR CANNED FRUIT

B **Analyze a Menu.** Look at the menu above. Answer the questions with a partner.

1. Who uses this menu?

2. What is the school serving on Monday?

3. Compare the menu to the pyramid on page 36. Does each meal include foods from each category?

4. How does this menu compare with your school's menu? Are the meals in your school the same, less healthy, or healthier than these meals?

5. Do you think you would like to eat at East Side High School? Why or why not?

A **Read.** Read the business letter of complaint about nutrition at East Side High School.

625 Caballo Lane
Amarillo, TX 65331
October 23, 2009

Food Services Department
East Side High School
3 East Side Drive
Amarillo, TX 65332

Dear Food Services Director:

I am writing to inform you of my concerns about the school lunches offered at East Side High School. As a nutritionist and a parent, I understand and care a lot about adolescent, or teenage, nutrition.

The lunches that you are currently offering in East Side High School's cafeteria are not well-balanced, adequate, or healthy meals. According to the United States Department of Agriculture (USDA), adolescents, like all of us, need healthy diets to function properly. The USDA recommends that adolescents eat whole grains, fresh fruits and vegetables, protein, and dairy products at each meal. The USDA discourages eating hydrogenated fats and oils and sweets.

East Side High's lunch menu does not comply with the USDA recommendations. Refined wheat flour, which is not a whole grain, is used in all the grains offered at East Side High. The fruits are not fresh, but either canned in syrup (a sweet) or offered as juice (no fiber). The proteins generally contain hydrogenated fats and oils. And sweets are offered at every meal. Students cannot function properly with this inadequate nutrition.

I realize that you have a small amount of money to spend on preparing meals. However, I think you can prepare tasty, healthy, and nutritious meals for the same price. Please read a nearby school's menu that I've included for your reference with this letter. I ask you to take our students' nutrition seriously. I expect that once you have examined the USDA recommendations and the other school's menu, you will make changes to East Side High's menu.

I look forward to next month's menu. I hope to see the refined grains replaced by whole grains and the fruits and desserts to be modified as well. I plan to send my letter and your response to the town newspaper. I am sure the town will be pleased to see your efforts.

Sincerely,

James Chalmers

Enclosures

Central High School Lunch Menu
September 2009

Monday	Baked Breaded Chicken with Whole Grain Roll Rice Cranberry Sauce
Tuesday	Hamburger or Cheeseburger on a Bun Corn Sliced Pears
Wednesday	Macaroni and Cheese with Whole Grain Roll Broccoli Fresh Orange
Thursday	Peanut Butter and Jelly Sandwich Carrot & Celery Sticks with Dressing Fresh Grapes
Friday	Slice of Cheese Pizza Garden Salad with Dressing Applesauce

B **Compare and Contrast.** **Compare and contrast Central High School's menu above with Eastside High's menu on page 37. Answer the questions with a partner.**

1. Look at Monday's meal on both menus. Which is healthier? Why?

2. Does Central High have more or fewer foods from each category on the pyramid?

3. How are the menus and meals similar at both schools? How are they different?

4. Would you rather eat at Central High or Eastside High? Why?

VOCABULARY

A Find each word in the reading on page 38. Look at the words around it to guess the meaning. Compare your answers with a partner.

Nouns	Adjectives	Adverb	Verbs
concern	adequate	properly	comply
department	inadequate		discourage
director	modified		examine
effort	offered		function
recommendation			inform
response			modify
service			recommend

B Match the word with its definition. Write the definition next to the words.

1. modify _____ *h. to change* _____
2. offer _____
3. examine _____
4. department _____
5. effort _____
6. response _____
7. service _____
8. adequate _____
9. inform _____
10. function _____

a. an answer
b. to study or look at carefully
c. to work correctly
d. a group or division
e. a try
f. sufficient
g. to tell or explain
h. ~~to change~~
i. act done for others
j. to make available

C Answer these questions using the vocabulary words from the box in activity A.

1. Who organizes and controls an event, a company, or a department?
2. Which two words are antonyms, or opposites?
3. When you do what you are asked or told to do, you do what?
4. What two words in the box can be both a verb and a noun without changing its form?
5. What word means the opposite of *encourage*?
6. How are things done when they are done in the right way?
7. What is another word for *fears* or *worries*?
8. When you make suggestions, what do you do?

Present Tense vs. Present Continuous Tense		
Present	**Present Continuous**	**Sentence with Present Continuous**
write	am writing	I am writing to inform you of my concerns.
offer	are offering	The lunches that you are offering are inadequate.

The present continuous tense is used to tell what is happening right now, in this moment.
To form the present continuous tense, you use a form of the verb *to be: am, is, are*.
Then add *–ing* to the end of the main verb. *Write* becomes *am writing*.
Remember to drop the *e* at the end of some verbs before adding *–ing*.

A Complete the sentences with the present continuous tense form of the verbs in the box. Use each verb only once.

offer   try   learn   modify   take   enjoy

1. Now our high school _____*is offering*_____ health and nutrition classes during the school day.

2. I _____ a nutrition and exercise class.

3. At first I was nervous, but now I _____ the class.

4. We _____ so much about healthy diets and proper exercise.

5. Now my friends and I _____ our diets.

6. Also, we _____ to walk to and from school more often.

Sentences with Adjective Clauses with *that*, *which*, and *who*	
Relative Pronoun	**Sentence with Adjective Clause**
which	The lunches, **which** you are currently offering, are inadequate.
that	The school **that** my child attends is called Eastside High.
who	The parent **who** is writing the letter is also a nutritionist.
that	The parent **that** is writing the letter is also a nutritionist.

Adjective clauses are phrases that modify, or tell more about, a noun. They often begin with the relative pronouns *that, which,* and *who. That, which,* and *who* refer to the subject of a sentence. *Which* refers to nonliving objects or animals. Clauses with *which* usually give information that is not essential to the meaning of the sentence. Use commas before and after the adjective clause to show that it is not essential to the meaning of the sentence. *Who* refers to people. *That* can refer to either living or nonliving objects, animals, or people.

B Read each pair of sentences. Then combine them using *that*, *which*, or *who* in an adjective clause. You may need to delete some words when you combine the sentences.

1. We are sorry to tell you. The company is now out of business.
   We are sorry to tell you that the company is now out of business.

2. We are sending back the product. The product no longer works.
   _____

3. I would like to speak with the sales person. The sales person helped me.
   _____

4. We would like a refund. The refund is why we are writing.
   _____

5. We would like to inform you. The product broke in the mail.
   _____

ORGANIZATION

Order of Importance

Complete the outline with information from the letter on page 38.

> **Remember!**
> **Business letters** are usually organized in **order of importance**. This means that the writer tells the most important information first. All the less important information follows. One type of business letter is a **letter of complaint** .

James's Letter of Complaint

I. Reasons for writing the letter—what James wants:

  A. To tell the reader: **1.** _____ *about school lunch nutrition at East Side High* _____

  B. To ask the reader: **2.** _____

II. Compare and Contrast—what James expected:

  A. What did James expect? **3.** _____

  B. Why did James expect this? **4.** _____

III. Compare and Contrast—what the reality is:

  A. What is the reality? **5.** _____

  B. How does it compare with James's expectations? **6.** _____

IV. Closing—what can be done about it:

  A. What suggestions does James make? **7.** _____

V. Closing—how James will follow up:

  B. What will James do to make sure his suggestions are considered?

    8. _____

WRITING STRATEGIES

Register

A Read the pairs of sentences or phrases. Write *business* next to the formal sentences or phrases and *personal* next to the informal ones. Please check format for capitals here.

1. A. Dear John, _____*personal*_____

    B. Dear Mr. Robertson: _____*business*_____

2. A. Love, _____

    B. Sincerely, _____

3. A. Could you send me a new model? _____

    B. I am writing to request a new model. _____

4. A. Please inform me of your return policy. _____

    B. What's your return policy? _____

5. A. I understand that you are offering replacements for broken products.

        _____

    B. Someone told me that you're giving replacements for broken products.

        _____

6. A. Please help me. _____

    B. I would appreciate your help. _____

Compare and Contrast

B Re-read the second and third paragraphs in the letter on page 38. What does the nutritionist/USDA expect? What is the reality? List your findings in the chart. Please double-check text format in box below

Nutritionist/USDA expects		Reality
whole grains	1.	*refined wheat flour*
fresh fruits	2.	
3.		hydrogenated fats and oils
few sweets	4.	

Business Letter Forms

Write the following information on the top of the business letter and the envelope provided.

Sender: Carlos Santoyo 2539 Olive Avenue Burbank CA 91502
Receiver: Musical Instruments for Beginners Human Resources Department 1500 North Verdugo Road Glendale CA 91208
Date: March 5, 2009

1. _____ Sender
2. _____ Sender's address
3. _____

4. _____ Receiver of letter (company)
5. _____ Department/person
6. _____ Street address
7. _____ City/State/ZIP code

Sender's address 8. _____
9. _____
Date 10. _____

Company 11. _____
Department/person 12. _____
Receiver's address 13. _____
14. _____

Dear Human Resources Manager:

Body Paragraphs

Closing 15. _____
Signature 16. _____

Business Letter of Complaint

A business letter is different from a composition. It is usually brief, direct, and very limited in its subject. Basically, you tell your purpose and what you want, explain why, make any other requests, and close. The language of all business letters is formal and polite. It can be about a service or a product. Letters of complaint usually have three main paragraphs. In the first paragraph, you tell what you want and why. For letters of complaint about products, you also include a detailed description of the product and tell when and where it was used or purchased. In the second (and sometimes third) paragraph, you compare and contrast what was promised or expected with the reality, citing specific examples or reasons. In the last paragraph(s), you make suggestions or demands and tell how you will follow-up or check that the demands are fulfilled.

 Read. Read Diya's letter of complaint.

105 Forest Street
Stoneham, MA 01880
May 10, 2009

Long Kicks
Customer Service Office
1 Kicks Drive
Shrewsbury, MA 02135

Dear Customer Service Representative:

   I am writing to inform you of my disappointment in your Long Kicks sneakers. On April 25, 2009, I bought a pair of Long Kicks sneakers at Smart Sporting Goods store. They are white with black stripes, women's size 7. The model number is LK5334.

   Unfortunately, your product has not performed well, because in just two weeks, the sneakers have fallen apart. I am disappointed because your advertisements show teenagers like me playing while wearing the sneakers. The advertisements also promise that Long Kicks sneakers will last as long as I need them. I wore the new pair of Long Kicks sneakers for two weeks. During that time, I went to school, played sports, and spent time outside. I expected the sneakers to last me at least several months, as other sneakers have. I do not consider two weeks to be "as long as I need them."

   To resolve the problem, I would appreciate your sending me a new pair of Long Kicks that have been checked for quality assurance. Enclosed are copies of a picture of my "new" Long Kicks, my receipt, and one of your advertisements.

   I look forward to your reply and a resolution to my problem. I will wait until June 15, 2009 before seeking help from a consumer protection agency or the Better Business Bureau. Please contact me at the above address or by phone at 555-879-3459.

Sincerely,

Diya Patel
Enclosures

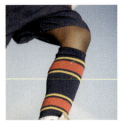

If you play hard, you need sneakers that play even harder. Long Kicks: sneakers that last as long as you need them.

SMART SPORTING GOODS

9 00000 00000 3 (81000 00000

LONG KICKS WOMEN'S SNEAKERS
B&W/Size 7
MODEL #   LK5334
=================================
TOTAL $▓▓.▓▓

STEP-BY-STEP WRITING

Purpose: Write a Letter of Complaint

WRITING PROMPT

Think of a product or service that has been inadequate. Write a three-paragraph letter of complaint to the company or person that is responsible for the product or service. Tell why you are unhappy with it. Compare and contrast your expectations with the reality. Make suggestions and tell how you will follow up.

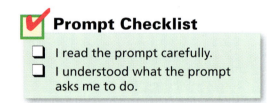 **Prompt Checklist**

❑ I read the prompt carefully.
❑ I understood what the prompt asks me to do.

STEP 1 Pre-write

Look at Diya's notes about her sneakers. Make your own notes about the product or service that you found to be inadequate. Describe the product or service in as much detail as you can. If possible, gather the product, an advertisement, a receipt, and any other important information. Describe each item you gathered in detail and tell how it is important to your complaint.

Why am I writing? I want to tell Long Kicks that I am unsatisfied with their sneakers.

The product: white with black stripes, women's size 7, Model number LK5334 Now they

are totally falling apart. My toe is poking through the front of the sneaker. The back

of the sole is coming apart.

The advertisement: Shows a teenager being rough with Long Kicks. Tells that Long Kicks

will last as long as I need them.

Receipt: April 25, 2009 Smart Sporting Goods store.

What I want from Long Kicks: new sneakers that will last longer, that have been checked

for quality. I want them quickly as I can't wear these Long Kicks much longer.

How will I follow-up: If they don't send me new sneakers by next month, I will call the

Better Business Bureau or another consumer aid company.

STEP 2 Organize

Look at Diya's outline. Make your own outline for your letter.

Diya's Notes

Title: Letter of Complaint about Long Kicks Sneakers

I. **Reasons for writing the letter—what I want:**
  A. To tell the reader: I am disappointed with Long Kicks sneakers.
  B. Product description: On April 25, 2009, I bought a pair of Long Kicks sneakers at Smart Sporting Goods store, white with black stripes, women's size 7. The model number is LK5334.

II. **Compare and Contrast—what I was promised/expected:**
  A. The ads say: "Long Kicks will last as long as you need them." They lasted two weeks.
  B. I expected them to last several months: They lasted two weeks.

III. **Closing—what can be done about it:**
  A. I want: a new pair of Long Kicks that have been checked for quality assurance.
  B. Follow-up: I will wait until June 15, 2009 before seeking help from a consumer protection agency or the Better Business Bureau; contact information: the above address or phone 555-879-3459.

STEP 3 Draft and Revise

A **Practice.** Look at Diya's first draft. How can she improve it? Answer the questions on page 49.

First Draft

(1) 105 Forest Street
(2) Stoneham, MA 01880
(3) May 10, 2009

(4) 1 Kicks Drive
(5) Shrewsbury, MA 02135
(6) Long Kicks
(7) Customer Service Office

(8) Dear Customer Service Representative:

(9) I am writing to inform you of my disappointment in your Long Kicks sneakers. (10) On April 25, 2009, I bought a pair of Long Kicks sneakers at Smart Sporting Goods store. (11) They are white with black stripes, women's size 7. (12) The model number is LK5334.

(13) To resolve the problem, I would appreciate your sending me a new pair of Long Kicks that have been checked for quality assurance. (14) Enclosed are copies of a picture of my "new" Long Kicks, my receipt, and one of your advertisements.

(15) Unfortunately, your product has not performed well, because in just two weeks, the sneakers have fallen apart. (16) I am disappointed because your advertisements show teenagers like me playing while wearing the sneakers. (17) The advertisements also promise. (18) Long Kicks sneakers will last as long as I need them. (19) I wore the new pair of Long Kicks sneakers for two weeks. (20) During that time, I went to school, played sports, and spent time outside.

(21) I want a reply and a resolution to my problem. (22) Please contact me at the above address or by phone at 555-879-3459.

(23) Sincerely,

Diya Patel

Enclosures

---

1. How can Diya address the letter correctly?
   A reorder lines 1–3 to be 3, 2, 1
   B reorder lines 1–3 to be 2, 3, 1
   C reorder lines 4–7 to be 6, 7, 4, 5
   D reorder lines 4–7 to be 5, 4, 7, 6

2. How can Diya better order her paragraphs to organize by order of importance?
   A reorder the paragraphs to be A, C, B, D
   B reorder the paragraphs to be B, A, C, D
   C reorder the paragraphs to be C, B, A, D
   D reorder the paragraphs to be A, D, C, B

3. How can Diya BEST combine sentences 17 and 18 to make a complex sentence with a relative pronoun?
   A The advertisements also promise which Long Kicks sneakers will last as long as I need them.
   B The advertisements, which also promise Long Kicks sneakers will last as long as I need them.
   C The advertisements also promise that Long Kicks sneakers will last as long as I need them.
   D The advertisements also promise, Long Kicks sneakers will last as long as I who need them.

4. Which sentences can Diya BEST add after sentence 20 to compare and contrast expectations with reality?
   A I expected the sneakers to last me at least several months, as other sneakers have. I do not consider two weeks to be "as long as I need them."
   B I want the sneakers to last me at least several months, as other sneakers have. You promise that they would last "as long as I need them."
   C The sneakers are falling apart. I can barely wear them anymore.
   D Now I need new sneakers. I expect you to send me newer and better sneakers.

5. How can Diya BEST rewrite sentence 21 to be in polite, formal language?
   A I want you to reply and solve my problem.
   B I need a reply and a resolution to my problem.
   C You should give me a reply and a resolution to my problem.
   D I look forward to your reply and a resolution to my problem.

6. Which sentence should Diya add after sentence 21 to show that she will take more serious action if required?
   A I will wait until June 15, 2009 before seeking help from a consumer protection agency or the Better Business Bureau.
   B I hope that you will follow my suggestions.
   C I am seriously disappointed.
   D I will never buy Long Kicks sneakers again and I will recommend the same course of action to all my friends and family members.

B **Draft.** Write a first draft of your letter of complaint. Use your notes from Steps 1 and 2.

C **Revise.** Read your first draft. How can you improve it? Look at the revision checklist. Revise your writing.

STEP 4 Edit

A **Practice.** Look at the sentences. Choose the best word or phrase to complete each sentence.

1. I _____ to inform you of my disappointment with your product.
   A was writing
   B am writing *(circled)*
   C wrote
   D write

2. Right now, my family and I _____ to use your product.
   A am trying
   B are trying
   C were trying
   D tries

3. We hope _____ you will send us a new product.
   A that
   B which
   C who
   D if

4. The woman _____ sold me the product was not polite.
   A which
   B if
   C who
   D after

5. The repairperson _____ to our house in a few minutes.
   A came
   B are coming
   C is coming
   D come

6. The product _____ you sent is a disappointment.
   A if
   B who
   C that
   D after

7. _____ as soon as possible.
   A Contact me
   B Call
   C You should call
   D Please contact me

8. _____ a new product.
   A Please send me
   B I want
   C I need
   D You should send me

B **Edit.** Re-read your draft from Step 3. Look at the editing checklist. Edit your writing.

C **Peer Edit.** Exchange drafts with a partner. Tell your partner what you like about the draft. Look at the editing checklist. Tell your partner how to improve the draft.

Editing Checklist

me	my partner	
❏	❏	wrote the addresses correctly
❏	❏	used present and present continuous tenses correctly and when needed
❏	❏	wrote complex sentences with pronouns correctly
❏	❏	used polite, formal language

STEP 5 Publish

Rewrite your business letter of complaint in your best handwriting or use a computer. Look at Diya's letter on page 45 for ideas. Present your letter to the class.

TECHNOLOGY

Finding Consumer Protection Resources Online

- Go to an online search engine.

- Do a **keyword search** for consumer protection agencies.

- Before clicking on the Web sites you found, evaluate the source. Is it reliable? Most reliable sources are federal or state protection agencies. Can you find your service or product at a federal or state protection agency? If not, open and evaluate a *.com* or *.org* site. Does the person writing the site seem knowledgeable and unbiased?

- Read the site to find out what you can do about your inadequate service or product.

Unit 4

Define a Term

UNIT OBJECTIVES

Writing
definition essay

Organization
traditional vs. nontraditional
definition with two examples

Writing Strategies
connecting ideas

Writing Conventions
citing sources

Vocabulary
art words

Grammar
infinitives and gerunds
complex sentences
parallel structure

Technology
using online dictionaries
   and encyclopedias

Exaltation of the Flower *by an unknown
Greek carver*

Banana Flower by Georgia O'Keeffe

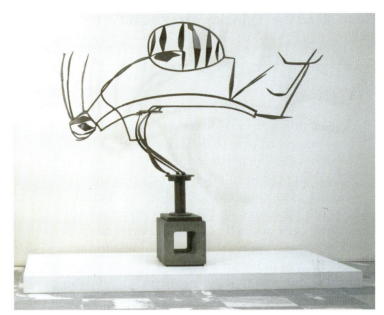

Australia by David Smith

 Analyze Artwork. Look at the artwork on this page and on page 52. Answer the questions about each picture with a partner.

1. What kind of artwork is this?

2. Describe the artwork. What do you see?

3. What do you think the artist is showing in the artwork?

4. Have you seen artwork like this before? Where?

5. What questions do you have about the artwork?

Read. Read the definition essay about art.

Art

Few words have as many definitions and as many people arguing to define it as the word *art*. Webster's Dictionary describes art as "a human skill of expression of other objects by painting, drawing, sculpting, etc." ("Art" 32). Art critics, museum directors, and gallery owners usually control how to define "skill." After all, not everyone who paints, draws, or sculpts can show work in a museum or gallery. A person's skills and techniques must be excellent. Artists also define art, for they are the ones who produce it. Finally, you and I, the observers of art, also say what we think is and is not art. Art can have both traditional and nontraditional definitions.

The first definition of art included the traditional idea that art is skillful, beautiful work that realistically shows the world around us. From the beginning of human history, artists have been trying to depict the world around them as realistically as possible (Stokstad xxxi). The Ancient Greeks told a story about two artists having a contest to see who could create the most realistic painting of a bowl of grapes. The first artist showed his painting, which was so realistic that birds flew down to peck at it. Then he turned to his rival and asked him to pull back the curtain hanging over his picture. His rival happily replied that there was no curtain. He had painted the curtain. The rival won because he had tricked a fellow artist by his realistic painting (Levy). Like the artists in the story, the Ancient Greek who carved a man and a woman looking at a flower made them as real as possible.

Not everyone agrees with the traditional definition of art. Leonardo da Vinci said that the artist who copied nature was only acting as a mirror. Da Vinci believed that art should be about ideas and feelings (Stokstad xxxi). This is called *abstract art*. Some abstract art is still about objects that we recognize, but the focus of the art

Shouting Warrior by Leonardo da Vinci

is on ideas or feelings. Georgia O'Keeffe shows her feelings through her painting of the flower on page 53. Other abstract art, which is often called *nonrepresentational art*, looks nothing like the objects in our world. This art shows only the inner world of thoughts or feelings. David Smith's sculpture on page 53 does not represent anything recognizable, but rather depicts Smith's inner world.

Although many people now use abstract or nonrepresentational definitions of art, some people continue to define art traditionally. Art is one of those words that maintains its old definition even as people continue to change it. The definition of art, like a work of art itself, can be interpreted by all who look at it.

Sources:

Levy, Daniel S. "Creating Grand Illusions." <u>Time</u>. 24 June 2001 <www.time.com/time/magazine/article/0,9171,1101901210-153313,00.html>.

Stokstad, Marilyn. <u>Art History</u>. Upper Saddle River, NJ: Pearson Prentice Hall, 2005.

"Art." <u>Webster's Dictionary</u>. Ashland, OH: Landoll, 1993.

VOCABULARY

A Find these words in the reading on page 54. Work with a partner to examine the use of each word and guess its meaning.

Adjectives	Verbs	Nouns	
abstract	define	critic	sculpture
nontraditional	depict	definition	skill
realistic	interpret	observer	technique
recognizable		rival	
traditional			

B Match the word with its definition.

1. definition ___*c. the meaning of a word*___

2. abstract _____

3. technique _____

4. sculpture _____

5. realistic _____

6. traditional _____

7. recognizable _____

8. observer _____

9. define _____

10. rival _____

a. a person who carefully watches the world around him- or herself

b. seeming genuine, true, or life-like

c. ~~the meaning of a word~~

d. a work of art created by shaping a material into another form

e. special method of doing something

f. a person who competes against another

g. passed down from generations

h. to give meaning to

i. easily identified

j. neither concrete nor realistic

C Answer these questions using the vocabulary words from the box in Activity A.

1. When you give the dictionary meaning of a word, what do you do?

2. What is the opposite of traditional?

3. Who is a person who carefully watches the world around him or her?

4. What is a synonym for *method*?

5. Who is someone who fights or competes against another?

6. When an artist shows something through art, what does the artist do?

7. Who are people who express their opinions about others or others' work?

8. When you give new meaning to a word or artwork, what do you do?

Infinitives and Gerunds		
Verb	**Infinitive**	**Gerund**
paint begin	to paint to begin	painting beginning

Gerunds (used as nouns) and infinitives are formed from verbs.

    gerund = verb + *-ing*

    infinitive = *to* + verb

Some verbs are usually followed by gerunds (***enjoy*** *dancing,* ***finish*** *studying,* ***suggest*** *hiking*).

Some expressions are often followed by gerunds (***tired of*** *waiting,* ***sorry about*** *forgetting,* ***interested in*** *learning*).

Other verbs are often followed by infinitives (***agree*** *to go,* ***plan*** *to travel,* ***want*** *to buy*).

A   Complete the sentences with the correct form of the verbs.

1. Ever since I was three years old, I have enjoyed _____*creating*_____ art. (to create / creating)

2. I plan _____ an artist when I graduate. (to be / being)

3. I hope _____ to college to study art. (to go / going)

4. I am most interested in _____ sculpture. (to study / studying)

5. My art teacher wants me _____ painting. (to consider / considering)

6. I am tired of _____ (to paint / painting) and want to learn to sculpt.

Complex Sentences		
Dependent Clause	**Independent Clause**	**Complex Sentence**
For they are the ones Who produce it	Artists also define art.	Artists also define art, **for** they are the ones **who** produce it.
Although many people now use abstract or nonrepresentational definitions of art	Some people continue to define art traditionally.	**Although** many people now use abstract or nonrepresentational definitions of art, some people continue to define art traditionally.

A complex sentence is made up of two or more dependent and independent **clauses**. A clause is a group of words with a subject and a verb. An independent clause is a complete sentence. A dependent clause is not a complete sentence. Clauses are joined by connecting words, such as *because, that, although, for, while, when, who.*

B Complete the answers according to the ideas and information from the reading on page 54. Your answers can be in your own words.

1. Why is it so difficult to define the word art?
   It is difficult to define art because *so many different people are trying to define it.*

2. Who defines art?
   They are people who _____.

3. How do some people define art?
   Some people define art traditionally while _____.

4. How do some people define art traditionally?
   They say that _____.

5. When does Leonardo da Vinci think art is just a mirror?
   He thinks it is a mirror when _____.

Parallel Structure	
Verb Form Agreement	**Nouns (Gerund) Form Agreement**
After all, not everyone who **paints, draws, or sculpts** can show work in a museum or gallery.	Webster's Dictionary describes art as "a human skill of expression of other objects by **painting, drawing, sculpting**, etc."

The verbs in a verb phrase must all agree, or be in the same form.
The nouns (or gerunds) in a noun phrase must all agree, too.

C Read each sentence. Correct the underlined phrase by rewriting the sentence.

1. In art class, we are studying famous <u>painters, sculptors, and other art</u>.
   In art class, we are studying famous painters, sculptors, and other artists.

2. First <u>we read about the artist, then we talk about the artist, and finally we try to create like the artist</u>.
   _____

3. I am studying the <u>paintings, drawings, and photograph</u> of Georgia O'Keeffe.
   _____

4. The way she <u>paints, drawing, and takes pictures</u> is incredible!
   _____

5. Someday, I hope <u>to paint, to draw, and taking photographs</u> like her.
   _____

6. Right now, I am just trying to learn about <u>her life, artwork, and creating</u>.
   _____

Definition Essay: Two Structures

Definition essays are usually organized in one of two ways: **traditional versus nontraditional** or **definition with two examples**.

Definition Essay	Traditional versus Nontraditional	Definition with Two Examples
Paragraph 1:	Both kinds of essays have an introduction paragraph in which the author introduces the term and gives a simple, dictionary definition of the term.	
Paragraph 2:	The author gives and explains the traditional definition of the term.	The author gives and explains one example of the term.
Paragraph 3:	The author gives and explains the nontraditional definition.	The author gives and explains another example of the term.
Paragraph 4:	Usually, but not always, there is a conclusion paragraph in both kinds of definition essays.	

The reading on page 54 shows the traditional versus nontraditional structure. Complete the outline with information from the reading.

Art

I. Introduction
   A. Dictionary definition: **1.** *"a human skill of expression of other objects by painting, drawing, sculpting, etc." (Webster's Dictionary)*
   B. Other introductory information: **2.** _____

II. Traditional Definition
   A. Traditional definition: **3.** _____
   B. Explanation/example: **4.** _____

III. Nontraditional Definition
   A. Abstract art definition: **5.** _____
      1. Explanation/example: **6.** _____
   B. Nonrepresentational art definition: **7.** _____
      1. Explanation/example: **8.** _____

IV. Conclusion
   A. Conclusion information: **9.** _____

WRITING STRATEGIES

Connecting Ideas

Complete the sentences with the connecting words from the box.

> that   ~~as~~   when   while   who

1. Some words change in definition _____*as*_____ people in a society change.

2. Some people define art traditionally _____ others define it nontraditionally.

3. Many people use both definitions _____ they talk about art.

4. Many people believe _____ art should be beautiful.

5. They are artists, critics, and gallery owners _____ define art traditionally.

WRITING CONVENTIONS

Citing Sources

See the Citation Guide found in the Writer's Reference on page 180 for information on how to create a Works Cited list.

Look at the reading on page 54. Find examples of parenthetical citations. Answer the questions below.

1. Which dictionary did the author use to define art? _____*Webster's*_____

2. On what page did the author find the definition? _____

3. What information did the author find in the book *Art History*? _____

4. Where did the author find the story of the two competing Ancient Greek painters? _____

WRITING

Definition Essay

A **definition essay** is a nonfiction text, usually three to five paragraphs long, and all about one term or idea. This kind of essay gives and explains the dictionary definition for the term. Then it offers either a traditional/nontraditional examination of the term or examples and explanations of the term. Definition essays are often found in brochures, magazine or newspaper articles, and textbooks.

 A **Read.** Read Sonali's definition essay on culture.

Culture

by Sonali Gopal

Everyone belongs to at least one culture. Most people belong to many cultures. For example, I was born in India, so the foods I eat and the clothes I wear are often from my Indian culture. However, I live in the United States, so I learn in U.S. schools and watch U.S. movies and television. I also belong to the world-wide culture through the Internet. So what exactly is culture? *The World Book Multimedia Encyclopedia* states that, "cultural traits can be divided into material culture and nonmaterial culture" ("Culture"). Material culture is all the things that are made by the members of a society—food, clothes, and other goods. Nonmaterial culture is the society's behaviors and beliefs—how we greet each other and what we believe about love, for example. Cultures throughout the world have differences and share similarities in their material and nonmaterial traits.

Material culture is the objects of a culture. Buildings, fashion, and art are just some examples of material culture. Look around you. The way the houses, apartments, and buildings look are part of your culture. In other parts of the country and in other parts of the world, people build their buildings differently. All people make homes, but the way they make them shows their culture. The material culture of a society is often due to available resources. For example, one culture may make jewelry from shells and shark's teeth because they live near the ocean. Even the art or music produced by a culture is affected by what is available. Some people have electricity, computers, and recording equipment. They create electronic music. People also buy or borrow resources from other cultures to create new material objects.

Nonmaterial culture is the ideas and beliefs of a culture. Learning, language, and customs are some examples of nonmaterial culture. All people learn. Some cultures have elaborate systems of education from preschool through college. Other cultures have more simple ways of teaching through daily eating, working, and family living. All people use language. Yet some people who speak the same language have very different cultural customs. For example, people in both the United States and England speak English. However, many people in England eat smoked fish for breakfast while most people in the United States eat cereal in the morning. Customs are the way people from a culture do things ("Custom" 103). How and what you eat are part of your culture.

In the United States, we are multicultural. This means that many cultures exist with and are enriched by each other. Some of the customs, beliefs, and ideas in our homes may be different from those in our neighbors' homes. However, as we share our cultures, we learn new ways of thinking, acting, and doing. We grow as the definition of our culture grows.

Sources:
"Culture." World Book Multimedia Encyclopedia. Chicago: World Book, Inc., 2007.
"Custom." The American Heritage Dictionary. Boston: Houghton Mifflin Company, 1985.

B **Summarize.** Reread Sonali's essay on culture on page 60. Summarize each paragraph below the correct group of pictures. The first one has been done for you.

I.

  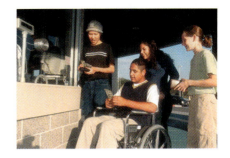

Sonali is Indian and lives in the United States. Her food and clothing are often Indian, but her school, TV, and movies are American. Culture is the material and nonmaterial parts of a group of people.

II.

_____

_____

III.

_____

_____

IV.

_____

_____

 C **Identify Form.** Re-read Sonali's essay on culture on page 60. Discuss the following questions with a partner.

1. What are paragraphs 2 and 3 about?

2. What kind of description essay is this: traditional/nontraditional or definition/examples?

3. What is the evidence in the essay that shows what form it is?

STEP-BY-STEP WRITING

Purpose: Define a Term

WRITING PROMPT

Choose a word that has more than one definition. Write a four-paragraph definition essay about that term. Choose either the traditional/nontraditional form or definition/examples form. Share your essay with your classmates.

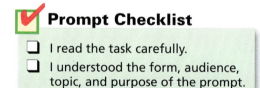 **Prompt Checklist**

❑ I read the task carefully.
❑ I understood the form, audience, topic, and purpose of the prompt.

STEP 1 Pre-write

A Look at Sonali's list of words that are difficult to define. Make your own list of words. Think about your culture. Is there a point of general disagreement between people of your age and people of your parents' or grandparents' age? Or write about words that have changed for _you_. How did you define these words? How do you define them now?

home	success	traditions
ancestor	discrimination	culture
money	teenager	criticism

B After you have chosen a word, list all the words and phrases that come to mind when you think about this word. Go over your list and circle the things you want to include in your essay. Also, look up and record the dictionary definition of the word.

Culture

(clothing)	(language)	family activities	(food)
(movies)	(school)	jobs	(beliefs)
pastimes	religion	(jewelry)	(TV)
sports	(eating habits)	art	(Internet)
(fashion)	bed times	(music)	(customs)

"Cultural traits can be divided into material culture and nonmaterial culture."—World Book

STEP 2 Organize

Look at Sonali's outline. Decide if you are writing in a traditional/nontraditional or a definition/examples form. Make your own outline about the word you chose.

Sonali's Outline

Title: Culture
(Definition/2 Example Form)

  I. Introduction
    A. People can belong to many cultures.
      1. My cultures: Indian and American
    B. Definition of culture: material and nonmaterial from World Book

  II. Body 1
    A. Examples of material culture
      1. Buildings
      2. Fashion
      3. Art

  III. Body 2
    A. Examples of nonmaterial culture
      1. Learning
      2. Language
      3. Customs

  IV. Conclusion
    A. United States as multicultural
      1. Include the reader in defining culture.

Practice. Look at Sonali's first draft. How can she improve it? Answer the questions.

First Draft
Culture
by Sonali Gopal

(1) Everyone belongs to at least one culture. (2) Most people belong to many cultures. (3) For example, I am born in India, so the foods I eat and the clothes I wear are often from my Indian culture. (4) However, I live in the United States, so I learn in U.S. schools and watch U.S. movies and television. (5) I also belong to the world-wide culture through the Internet. (6) So what exactly is culture? (7) *The World Book Multimedia Encyclopedia* states that, "cultural traits can be divided into material culture and nonmaterial culture ("Culture"). (8) Material culture is all the things that are made by the members of a society-food, clothes, and other goods. (9) Nonmaterial culture is the society's behaviors and beliefs-how we greet each other and what we believe about love, for example. (10) Cultures throughout the world have differences and share similarities in their material and nonmaterial traits.

(11) Material culture is the objects of a culture. (12) Buildings, fashion, and art are just some examples of material culture. (13) Look around you. (14) The way the houses, apartments, and buildings look are part of your culture. (15) In other parts of the country and in other parts of the world, people build their buildings differently. (16) All people make homes, but the way they make them shows their culture. (17) The material culture of a society is often due to available resources. (18) For example, one culture may make jewelry from shells and shark's teeth. (19) They live near the ocean. (20) Even the art or music produced by a culture is affected by what is available. (21) Some people have electricity, computers, and recording equipment. (22) They create electronic music. (23) People also buy or borrow resources from other cultures to create new material objects.

(24) Nonmaterial culture is the ideas and beliefs of a culture. (25) Learning, language, and customs are some examples of nonmaterial culture. (26) All people learn. (27) Some cultures have elaborate systems of education from preschool through college. (28) Other cultures have more simple ways of teaching through daily eating, working, and family living. (29) All people use language. (30) Yet some people who speak the same language have very different cultural customs. (31) For example, people in both the United States and England speak English. (32) However,

many people in England eat smoked fish for breakfast.
(33) Most people in the United States eat cereal in the morning.
(34) Customs are the way people from a culture do things-"Custom"
103. (35) How and what you eat are part of your culture.

(36) In the United States, we are multicultural. (37) This
means that many cultures exist with and are enriched by each other.
(38) Some of the customs, beliefs, and ideas in our homes may be
different from those in our neighbors' homes. (39) However, as we
share our cultures, we learn new ways of thinking, acting, and
doing. (40) We grow as the definition of our culture grows.

1. How can Sonali correct sentence 3?
   (A) Change *am born* to *was born*.
   B Change *clothes* to *cloth*.
   C Change *I wear* to *I am wearing*.
   D Change *I eat* to *I ate*.

2. What is the main idea of paragraph 2?
   A Cultures are different all over the world.
   B Cultures are different throughout the United States.
   C The material forms of culture are things like buildings, fashion, and art.
   D The nonmaterial forms of culture are things like learning, language and customs.

3. Which word would best connect sentences 18 and 19 to make them one sentence?
   A but
   B because
   C and
   D although

4. What is the best way to combine sentences 32 and 33?
   A However, many people in England eat smoked fish for breakfast although most people in the United States eat cereal in the morning.
   B However, many people in England eat smoked fish for breakfast while most people in the United States eat cereal in the morning.
   C However, many people in England eat smoked fish for breakfast because most people in the United States eat cereal in the morning.
   D However, many people in England eat smoked fish for breakfast after most people in the United States eat cereal in the morning.

5. How can Sonali correct sentence 34?
   A Change *things—"Custom" 103.* to *things.—"Custom" 103*
   B Change *things—"Custom" 103.* to *things "Custom" 103.*
   C Change *things—"Custom" 103.* to *things. "Custom" 103*
   D Change *things—"Custom" 103.* to *things ("Custom" 103).*

B **Draft.** Write a first draft of your definition essay. Use your notes from Steps 1 and 2.

C **Revise.** Read your first draft. How can you improve it? Look at the revision checklist. Revise your writing.

STEP 4 Edit

A **Practice.** Read the sentences. Choose the best substitute for the underlined words. If the sentence is correct, choose "Make no change."

1. Some words are more difficult than others <u>explaining or defining</u>.
   A to explaining or defining
   Ⓑ to explain or define
   C explain or define
   D Make no change.

2. Some words are difficult <u>because</u> we have strong feelings about them.
   A but
   B although
   C after
   D Make no change.

3. We have strong <u>emotions and thinks</u> about the words *mother* or *father*.
   A emotions and thoughts
   B emoting and thoughts
   C emotes and thinking
   D Make no change.

4. Definitions of the words have changed <u>that</u> people and the world have changed.
   A although
   B after
   C as
   D Make no change.

5. Traditionally, the word *mother* meant both female parent and primary caregiver, or the person <u>who</u> cares for the children.
   A as
   B which
   C while
   D Make no change.

6. As society changes, our definitions <u>changed</u>.
   A are changing
   B change
   C were changing
   D Make no change.

7. As a result, we may need <u>creating</u> some new words.
   A create
   B creates
   C to create
   D Make no change.

8. *Collegiate Encyclopedia* describes tradition as "a ritual or other act that people have done for a long time and continue to do." <u>("Tradition" 119.)</u>
   A ("Tradition," 119)
   B ("Tradition" 119)
   C ("Tradition" 119).
   D Make no change.

B | **Edit.** Re-read your draft from Step 3. Look at the editing checklist. Edit your writing.

 C | **Peer Edit.** Exchange drafts with a partner. Tell your partner what you like about the draft. Look at the editing checklist. Tell your partner how to improve the draft.

Editing Checklist

me	my partner	
❏	❏	used parallel structure in all my sentences
❏	❏	used connecting words correctly to make complex sentences
❏	❏	cited my sources correctly
❏	❏	used simple past tense and past continuous tense correctly
❏	❏	used infinitives and gerunds correctly

STEP 5 Publish

Write your definition essay in your best handwriting or use a computer. Look at Sonali's definition essay on page 60 for ideas. Present your essay to the class.

TECHNOLOGY

Using Online Dictionaries and Encyclopedias

- Go to an online search engine.

- Do a **keyword search** for your term. If it is a two-word term, then try typing it in quotation marks.

- Before clicking on any Web site you found, evaluate its source. Is it reliable? Some online encyclopedias are created by anyone who wants to contribute to it. These entries are not monitored for accuracy. If you are unsure about the encyclopedia or dictionary you've found, go to the page and find the "about us" link. Read how the encyclopedia is created and monitored.

- Find at least two reliable sources.

GROUP WRITING

Work in a group to write about one of these topics. Follow the steps below.

1. Choose your topic.
2. Discuss and record information.
3. Do research if you need to.
4. Write a first draft.
5. Revise and edit the draft with your group.
6. Present your group's essay to the class.

Topic 1

Write a letter of complaint about a product or service with which you are dissatisfied. Write a three-paragraph letter of complaint to the company or person responsible for the product or service. Tell why you are dissatisfied with it. Compare and contrast your expectations with the reality. Make suggestions about how your situation can be improved. Tell how you will follow up.

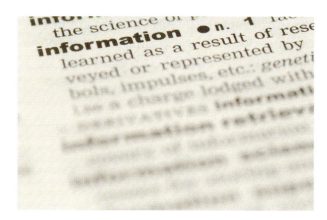

Topic 2

Choose any word that has more than one definition. Write a four-paragraph definition essay about that term. Choose either the traditional/nontraditional form or definition/examples form.

TIMED WRITING

Choose one writing prompt. Complete the writing task in 45 minutes.

WRITING PROMPT 1

Write a three-paragraph business thank-you letter to a person or company. Tell them how satisfied you are with their product or service. Compare and contrast your expectations with reality. Tell how you will buy or use the product or service in the future.

WRITING PROMPT 2

Choose one of the following words: *information, education, success, tradition, teenager, ancestor, criticism*. Write a four-paragraph definition essay about the word you chose. Choose either the traditional/nontraditional or definition/examples form.

 Test Tip

Voice! Remember to choose an appropriate tone for your draft. Think about who will read the draft. Choose formal or informal words and phrases.

SELF-CHECK

Think about your writing skills. Check (✔) the answers that are true.

1. I understand. . .
   - ❏ business complaint words.
   - ❏ art words.

2. I can correctly. . .
   - ❏ recognize and use different registers.
   - ❏ compare and contrast my expectations with the reality.
   - ❏ use connecting words to connect ideas.

3. I can correctly. . .
   - ❏ use present tense.
   - ❏ use present continuous tense.
   - ❏ write complex sentences with adjective clauses.
   - ❏ use infinitives and gerunds.
   - ❏ write complex sentences with connecting words.
   - ❏ use parallel structure.

4. I can correctly. . .
   - ❏ use business letter forms.
   - ❏ cite sources.

5. I can organize my writing. . .
   - ❏ by order of importance.
   - ❏ in traditional/nontraditional definition form.
   - ❏ in definition/examples form.

6. I can write to. . .
   - ❏ complain.
   - ❏ define.

Unit 5

Generalize Information

UNIT OBJECTIVES

Writing
general-to-specific essay

Organization
general to specific

Writing Strategies
drawing conclusions
words that signal examples

Writing Conventions
paraphrase information

Vocabulary
health words

Grammar
present perfect tense
linking verbs
demonstrative adjectives
and pronouns

Technology
using the Internet to research
examples

Elderly Japanese woman

Vegetarian food

Elderly exercise

 A **Analyze Photographs.** Look at the photographs on this page and on page 70. Answer the questions about each photograph with a partner.

1. What do the photographs show?

2. How are these photographs related to each other?

3. What is a general topic that might describe all of these photographs?

A **Read.** Read the general-to-specific essay about centenarians.

Centenarians

Some people live to be 100 years or older. They are called *centenarians*—people who live a century. Nearly every culture and country has centenarians. The islands off the coast of Japan called Okinawa have the most centenarians of any place in the world ("Investigating"). The island of Sardinia in Italy and the town of Loma Linda in California also have very high concentrations of centenarians. These centenarians not only live longer, but they also live much healthier lives, free of many of the normal complaints and diseases associated with old age. Scientists have begun to research why people who live in these parts of the world live longer, healthier lives.

Seiryu Toguchi is 103 years old. He lives in Okinawa, Japan, and is a good example of the centenarians who live there. He wakes up at 6:00 every morning. He stretches for a half hour. Then he eats a light breakfast, such as whole grain rice and soup with vegetables. For the rest of the morning, he works in his garden. At lunch, he eats stir-fried vegetables, egg, and tofu. Then he naps for an hour. He works in his fields for another two hours, then has dinner. Seiryu spends the evenings playing music before bed. He says he falls asleep thinking about all the things he wants to do the next day (Corliss). Scientists have found that genetics, or people's physical background, can affect longevity. But they now think that genetics account for only thirty percent of longevity (Buettner). Studies have shown that healthy eating, exercise, and low stress are the keys to a long, disease-free life ("Investigating").

Lifestyle is possibly the only explanation for the centenarians in Sardinia, Italy. Unlike anywhere else in the world, there are many male centenarians in Sardinia. Some scientists think this may be because most women are heads of the household in Sardinia. So men have less stressful lives. Sardinian centenarians, like those in Okinawa, grow much of their own food (Buettner). This provides them with beneficial exercise and highly nutritious food as well.

The highest concentration of centenarians in the United States is in Loma Linda, California (Buettner). Most of the people in this town practice a

Sardinia, Italy

religion that encourages its followers not to eat meat, drink alcohol, or smoke tobacco. Also, they are part of a supportive community and they live full, active lives. For example, Marge Gitan, who is 100 years old, weight lifts and rides a stationary bike every morning. She also plays tennis in tournaments. Marge still drives a car and provides rides for all of her less able (though younger) friends (Buettner). Like the centenarians in Okinawa and Sardinia, Marge and her centenarian friends in Loma Linda exercise, eat well, and live in strong communities.

The number of centenarians is growing worldwide because of healthier lifestyles, preventive medicine, and better healthcare. To illustrate, Seiryu Toguchi of Okinawa says that he goes to the doctor whenever he feels unwell, even if it is in the middle of the night (Corliss). Those who are very old and very healthy know how best to take care of themselves.

Sources:
Buettner, Dan. "The Secrets of Long Life." National Geographic. Nov. 2005. <www7.nationalgeographic.com/ngm/0511/sights_n_sounds/index.html>.
Okicent. Okinawan Centenarian Study. <www.okicent.org>.
Corliss, Richard and Michael D. Lemonick. "How to Live to Be 100." Time Magazine. 30 Aug. 2004. <http://www.time.com/time/magazine/article/0,9171,994967-7,00.html>.

VOCABULARY

A Find these words in the reading on page 72. Look at the words around it to guess the meaning. Compare your answers with a partner.

Adjectives		Nouns	Verbs
active	stationary	centenarian	account for
beneficial	supportive	complaints	encourage
male	unwell	diseases	weight lift
nutritious		healthcare	
preventive		longevity	

B Write the words from the box in the correct categories in the chart.

~~active~~	diseases	longevity	stationary	unwell
beneficial	encourage	nutritious	supportive	weight lift
~~complaints~~	healthcare	preventive		

Positive Health Words		Negative Health Words
active	_____	_complaints_
_____	_____	_____
_____	_____	_____
_____	_____	_____
_____	_____	_____

C Answer these questions using the vocabulary from the box in Activity A.

1. What is the opposite of *female*?

2. Who are people who live 100 years or more?

3. When you give a report or explanation for something, what do you do?

4. What is an antonym for the word *active*?

5. How do you describe food that is good for you?

6. What kind of healthcare tries to stop problems before they occur?

7. When you are caring and helpful, what are you?

8. What do you call something that is good for you?

Present Perfect Tense

Verb	Example Sentence
begin	Scientists **have begun** to research why people who live in these parts of the world live longer, healthier lives.
find	Scientists **have found** that genetics, or people's physical background, can affect longevity.

Use the present perfect tense to tell about actions that began in the past but continue into the present or are completed in the present.

The present perfect tense is formed with *has* or *have* and the past participle of the verb.

The past participle of verbs is formed by adding *–ed* to the stem (researched, studied, etc.—remember, you may need to change *y* to *i* first). However, many common past participles are irregular (begun, bought, etc.).

A Complete the sentences with the present perfect form of the verbs in parentheses.

1. Okinawans _____*have eaten*_____ vegetable soup, rice, and tofu for centuries. (eat)

2. For years, Seiryu _____ his own vegetables in his garden. (grow)

3. Scientists _____ that fresher vegetables are more nutritious. (discover)

4. My aunt _____ in Loma Linda, California, for ten years. (live)

5. She _____ many centenarians there. (meet)

6. I _____ her many times. (visit)

7. Each time I visit, I _____ surprised to meet so many active centenarians. (be)

8. From the Loma Linda centenarians, my family _____ to eat well, exercise, and be supportive. (learn)

Linking Verbs

Linking Verb	Example Sentence
be	Seiryu Toguchi **is** a centenarian.
feel	He **feels** healthy.

A linking verb connects the subject of the sentence with a noun or adjective that gives information about the subject. Linking verbs do not show action.

Seiryu Toguchi **is** a centenarian.   He **feels** healthy.

   ↓   ↓   ↓   ↓   ↓   ↓

subject linking adjective   subject linking adjective
         verb   verb

B Complete the sentences using the linking verbs from the box.

| ~~are~~ | seem | look | taste | turn | remain | feel | become |

1. Exercise and nutritious eating _____*are*_____ important for a healthy life.

2. People _____ and _____ better when they eat and exercise well.

3. Following an exercise routine may _____ difficult at first.

4. Some nutritious foods may _____ different until you get used to them.

5. However, healthy living will help you _____ a stronger, healthier person.

6. A workout and a good meal can _____ a bad day into a good one.

7. Exercise and nutrition _____ the most important parts of a healthy lifestyle.

Demonstratives	
Demonstrative Adjective	**Demonstrative Pronoun**
These centenarians not only live longer, but they also live much healthier lives, free of many of the normal complaints and diseases associated with old age.	**This** provides them with beneficial exercise and highly nutritious food as well.

Demonstratives are the words: *this, that, these,* and *those.*
They can be used as adjectives before nouns or as pronouns, or replacements for nouns.

C Complete the following sentences using demonstrative adjectives or pronouns.

1. _____*That*_____ woman over there is 100 years old.

2. _____ makes her a centarian.

3. _____ people here are her children, grandchildren, and great-grandchildren.

4. _____ is her birthday.

5. Don't you think _____ is incredible?

6. She has lived all _____ years and is still healthy and happy.

7. _____ is her motto: Eat, worry, and hurry little; exercise, sleep, and love lots.

8. I will try to live by _____ motto.

ORGANIZATION

General-to-Specific Essay

A Complete the outline below with information from the reading on page 72.

Remember!
A **five-paragraph essay** has an introduction paragraph, three body paragraphs, and a conclusion paragraph. In a **general-to-specific essay**, the introduction gives and explains the generalization, or general thought, about the topic. Each body paragraph gives and explains a specific example of the generalization. The conclusion summarizes the examples and relates them back to the generalization.

Centenarians

I. **Introduction**

   A. Generalization: **1.** _Nearly every culture and country has centenarians._

   B. Other introductory information: **2.** _____

II. **Body Paragraph 1**

   A. Example: **3.** _____

      1. information about the example: **4.** _____

      2. information about the example: **5.** _____

      3. information about the example: **6.** _____

III. **Body Paragraph 2**

   A. Example: **7.** _____

      1. information about the example: **8.** _____

      2. information about the example: **9.** _____

      3. information about the example: **10.** _____

IV. **Body Paragraph 3**

   A. Example: **11.** _____

      1. information about the example: **12.** _____

      2. information about the example: **13.** _____

      3. information about the example: **14.** _____

V. **Conclusion**

   A. Summary: **15.** _____

   B. Connection to the generalization: **16.** _____

B Reread the article on page 72. Answer the following questions in complete sentences.

1. Which is the most important sentence in the whole essay? Why is it the most important?
The most important sentence is "Scientists have begun to research why people who live in these parts
of the world live longer, healthier lives." This sentence is most important because it tells readers what
they will read about in the remaining paragraphs.

2. Which paragraph is more specific: paragraph 1 or paragraph 2?
_____

3. How many different examples does the writer give to support the generalization?
_____

4. How is the information in the conclusion different from the information in paragraphs 2, 3, and 4? Why do you think the writer put this information last?
_____
_____

WRITING STRATEGIES

Remember!
Readers **draw conclusions** by making sensible decisions based on details or facts in a reading. To draw a conclusion, ask yourself: How are these details or facts related? What do they mean?

Drawing Conclusions

Match the following generalizations with the specific examples below. Then discuss with a partner why each generalization is an appropriate conclusion.

> A. Men in Sardinia have low-stress lives.
> B. Okinawans have the highest percentage of centenarians in the world because they are the healthiest people in the world.
> C. There are more centenarians in Loma Linda, California, than in any other part of the United States because of the religion many people practice there.

1. Their religion teaches them not to eat meat, drink alcohol, or use tobacco products. These people also live in close-knit, caring communities. _____ C _____

2. There are more male centenarians in Sardinia, Italy. Women are the heads of households. Running a house can be a very stressful job. _____

3. These centenarians eat fresh vegetables and very little meat. They also often practice eating until they are only eighty percent full. Exercise is part of their lifestyle. They stretch, walk, and garden daily. Finally, they live in communities where people care for each other. _____

Words that Signal Examples

Skim the reading on page 72, looking for words that signal examples. Copy those sentences on the lines below.

the reading on page 72

> **Remember!**
> Use words to show that you are giving an example, such as: *for example, such as, including, for instance, like, to illustrate.*

1. such as: *Then he eats a light breakfast, such as whole grain rice and soup with vegetables.*

   _____

2. like: _____

   _____

3. for example: _____

   _____

4. to illustrate: _____

   _____

WRITING CONVENTIONS

> **Remember!**
> When citing examples, you can quote information directly or **paraphrase** information. To **paraphrase** means to put something into your own words.

Paraphrase Information

Read the quotes below. Then skim the reading on page 72 to find the paraphrases of the quotes. Record the paraphrase on the line.

the reading on page 72

1. "More people in Okinawa live to age 100 and beyond than in any other place in the world."

   The islands off the coast of Japan called Okinawa have the most centenarians of any place in the world.

   _____

2. "Studies have concentrated on the genetics, diets, exercise habits, and psychospiritual beliefs and practices of the Okinawan elders."

   _____

   _____

3. "Like the Sardinians, the Okinawans grow most of their food themselves."

   _____

   _____

4. "Genetics only account for about thirty percent of how long you live."

   _____

   _____

WRITING

General-to-Specific Essay

A **general-to-specific essay** is a nonfiction text, usually five paragraphs long. This kind of essay gives and explains a generalization or general statement. At the end of the introduction paragraph, there is a thesis, or main idea, statement that lists the three supporting examples that will be discussed. Then each body paragraph gives and explains one of the examples. General-to-specific essays are often found in magazine or newspaper articles and textbooks.

 A **Read.** Read Kenzo's essay about forms of communication.

New Forms of Communication

by Kenzo Watanabe

This is the technology age. More and more people are relying on technology for everyday living. Young people, especially teenagers, are using technology as a primary means of communication. Cell phones, instant messaging, and online social networks are three main ways people use technology to communicate with each other.

Cell, or cellular, phones have been around for dozens of years. However, each year they become more sophisticated and more popular. Essentially, cell phones are small devices that connect the user via satellite to nearly any other phone in the world. In 2006, 203 million people in the United States had cell phones. Nearly two billion people worldwide had them (Leo). Now the numbers have grown even larger. Most people who own cell phones believe they have made their lives easier. However, studies have shown that there is a high correlation between car accidents and cell phone use. Some U.S. states have even passed laws prohibiting cell phone use by drivers in cars (Leo). Also, many people find the use of cell phones in public annoying and rude. For example, they think that people who conduct loud, personal conversations in typically quiet places, like restaurants or movie theaters, abuse this convenient method of communication.

Instant messaging (IM) is a relatively new method of communication that has replaced e-mailing in many informal and some formal settings. IM is the instant exchange of typed messages between two users of the Internet. One user types a short, informal message, which instantly pops up in a small box on the computer screen of the other user. Because IM is instantaneous, it seems more like speech than e-mail. Some unique IM language conventions have developed. Abbreviations such as K for "OK" and LOL for "laugh out loud" make instant messaging even faster (Schirber). Emoticons, which are faces created out of standard keyboard characters, communicate emotions with a few strokes of the keys. To illustrate, :-) is a smiley face; ;-) is a wink; :-(is a frown; and |-O is a yawn (Schirber).

Online social networks have given people a new way to present themselves to the world. Online social networks are Internet sites where a user creates a profile and builds a personal network that connects him or her to other users. Currently in the United States there are tens of millions of users. Fifty-five percent of teenagers who are online use social networks (Lenhari). Like cell phones, online social networks have some dangers. Because some networks allow anyone to create or view a profile, users need to avoid putting identifiable

---

personal information on their page. All sites allow users to close their profile to strangers, helping users to protect themselves (Lenhari).

Despite their annoyances and dangers, new forms of communication allow people to stay connected in a more and more fragmented and busy world. Before electricity and technological devices, people dreamed that someday they would create machines that would make their lives easier. Now we live in the age of our ancestors' dreams. Forms of communication that are fast, easy, and able to change with these hectic times help even the busiest people communicate with those around them.

Sources:
Lenhari, Amanda and Mary Madden. "Social Networking Websites and Teens: An Orverview." <u>Pew Internet</u>. 1 Jan. 2007. Pew Trust. 19 July 2007 <http://www.pewinternet.org/PPF/r/198/report_display.asp>.
Leo, Peter. "Cell Phone Statistics that May Surprise You." <u>Pittsburgh Post Gazette</u>. 16 Mar. 2006. 21 July 2007 <http://www.post-gazette.com/pg/06075/671034-294.stm>.
Schirber, Michael. "Study: Instant Messaging is Surprisingly Formal :-)." <u>Live Science</u>. 1 Mar. 2005. Imaginova Corp. 20 July 2007 <http://www.livescience.com/technology/050301_internet_language.html>.

B Re-read Kenzo's essay on new forms of communication on page 79. Summarize each body paragraph below the correct group of pictures. The first has been done for you.

I.

Cell phones are a popular form of communication. They connect the user via satellite with any other phone in the world. Because cell phones are so convenient, sometimes people abuse them by driving with them, which can be dangerous, or talking on them in public places, which can be rude.

II.

_____

_____

_____

_____

_____

III.

_____

_____

_____

_____

_____

Purpose: Generalize Information

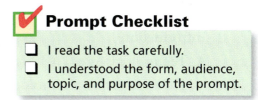

STEP 1 Pre-write

A Look at Kenzo's list of possible generalizations. Make your own list of generalizations. Imagine that you are a parent and think of the important lessons that you want to teach your children. Write them as generalizations. Make a list of generalizations that you can make from daily life. Make these generalizations from your experiences and from things friends and family members have told you.

Kenzo's List of Generalizations

The cost of healthcare is rising.	Tuition for college is going up.
Plants are important sources of medicines.	The quality of the products that we buy is going down.
New forms of communication make it easier for us to keep in touch.	An education is necessary for a good job.

B After you have chosen a generalization, list all the examples and specific details that come to mind when you think about this generalization. Go over your list and circle the three most compelling, or the three that you can explain the best.

Kenzo's List of Examples

New Forms of Communication		
cell phones	e-mail	MP3 players
text messaging	Web sites	online social networks
instant messaging	chat rooms	

STEP 2 Organize

Look at Kenzo's outline. Make your own outline about the generalization you chose.

Kenzo's Outline

Title: New Forms of Communication

I. **Introduction**

    A. Technology Age

        1. People using technology to communicate.

        2. Teens relying on technology to communicate.

    B. Thesis Statement: Cell phones, instant messaging, and online social networks are three main ways people use technology to communicate with each other.

II. **Body 1**

    A. Cell Phones

        1. What are they: phones that connect user via satellite to any phone in the world.

        2. Positive: can be used virtually anywhere, so people stay connected everywhere.

        3. Negative: can be dangerous when used by drivers and can be rude when used in certain public places.

III. **Body 2**

    A. Instant Messaging

        1. What it is: users send a message that instantly pops up on other user's computer screen.

        2. New language has formed: abbreviations and emoticons.

IV. **Body 3**

    A. Online Social Networks

        1. What it is: a user creates a profile and builds a personal network that connects him or her to other users.

        2. Who is using: U.S. has millions of users. 55% of online teens use social networks.

V. **Conclusion**

    A. Stay Connected

        1. In a busy world, these new forms keep us connected.

        2. Past people dreamed of technologies that would give us more time.

        3. Do we have more free time? No, but we are using these technologies to stay connected.

STEP 3 Draft and Revise

 A **Practice.** Look at Kenzo's first draft. How can he improve it? Answer the questions.

First Draft
New Forms of Communication
by Kenzo Watanabe

(1) Now is the technology age. (2) More and more people are relying on technology for everyday living. (3) Young people, especially teenagers, are using technology as a primary means of communication. (4) Cell phones, instant messaging, and online social networks are three main ways people use technology to communicate with each other.

(5) Cell, or cellular, phones are around for dozens of years. (6) However, each year they become more sophisticated and more popular. (7) Essentially, cell phones are small devices that connect the user via satellite to nearly any other phone in the world. (8) In 2006, 203 million people in the United States had cell phones. (9) Nearly two billion people worldwide had them (Leo). (10) Now the numbers have grown even larger. (11) Most people who own cell phones believe they have made their lives easier. (12) However, studies have shown that there is a high correlation between car accidents and cell phone use. (13) Some U.S. states have even passed laws prohibiting cell phone use by drivers in cars (Leo). (14) Also, many people find the use of cell phones in public annoying and rude. (15) They think that people who conduct loud, personal conversations in typically quiet places, like restaurants or movie theaters, abuse this convenient method of communication.

(16) Instant messaging (IM) is a relatively new method of communication that has replaced e-mailing in many informal and some formal settings. (17) One user types a short, informal message, which instantly pops up in a small box on the computer screen of the other user. (18) It seems more like speech than e-mail. (19) Some unique IM language conventions have developed. (20) Abbreviations such as K for "OK" and LOL for "laugh out loud" make instant messaging even faster (Schirber). (21) Emoticons, which are faces created out of standard keyboard characters, communicate emotions with a few strokes of the keys. (22) To illustrate, :-) is a smiley face; ;-) is a wink; :-(is a frown; and |-O is a yawn (Schirber).

(23) Online social networks have given people a new way to present themselves to the world. (24) Online social networks are Internet sites where a user creates a profile and builds a personal network that connects him or her to other users. (25) Currently in the United States there are tens of millions of users. (26) "More than half (55%) of all online American youths ages 12-17 use online social networking sites, according to a new national survey of teenagers conducted by Pew Internet & American Life Project" (Lenhari). (27) Like cell phones, online social networks have some dangers. (28) Because some networks allow anyone to create or view a profile, users need to avoid putting identifiable personal information on their page. (29) All sites allow users to close their profile to strangers, helping users to protect themselves (Lenhari).

> (30) Despite their annoyances and dangers, new forms of communication allow people to stay connected in a more and more fragmented and busy world. (31) Before electricity and technological devices, people dreamed that someday they would create machines that would make their lives easier. (32) Now we live in the age of our ancestors' dreams. (33) Forms of communication that are fast, easy, and able to change with these hectic times help even the busiest people communicate with those around them.

1. How can Kenzo BEST rewrite sentence 1?
   - **(A)** Change *Now* to *This*.
   - **B** Change *Now* to *That*.
   - **C** Change *Now* to *These*.
   - **D** Change *Now* to *Those*.

2. How can Kenzo correct sentence 5?
   - **A** Change *are* to *is*.
   - **B** Change *are* to *were*.
   - **C** Change *are* to *have been*.
   - **D** Change *are* to *are being*.

3. Which word or phrase can Kenzo add to the beginning of sentence 15?
   - **A** Is like
   - **B** Including
   - **C** Such as,
   - **D** For example,

4. Which sentence should Kenzo add after sentence 16 to BEST explain his example?
   - **A** More teens use text messaging than instant messaging, but instant messaging is still important.
   - **B** I use instant messaging several times each day.
   - **C** IM is the instant exchange of typed messages between two users of the Internet.
   - **D** Many companies have even begun to encourage their employees to use IM to speed up communication.

5. What phrase can Kenzo add to the beginning of sentence 18 to improve it?
   - **A** Because IM is instantaneous,
   - **B** Because IM feels instantaneous,
   - **C** Because IM sounds instantaneous,
   - **D** Because IM becomes instantaneous,

B **Draft.** Write a first draft of your general-to-specific essay. Use your notes from Steps 1 and 2.

C **Revise.** Read your first draft. How can you improve it? Look at the revision checklist. Revise your writing.

Revision Checklist
- ❏ I included a thesis statement.
- ❏ I wrote an introduction, three body paragraphs, and a conclusion paragraph.
- ❏ I explained each example clearly.
- ❏ I paraphrased information correctly and cited my sources honestly.
- ❏ I used signal words to show when I was giving an example.

STEP 4 Edit

A **Practice.** Read the sentences. Choose the best substitute for the underlined words. If the sentence is correct, choose "Make no change."

1. Today we go to the pharmacy or drug store when we _____ sick.
   A is
   (B) are
   C seem
   D remain

2. But where did people get medicine before there were _____ stores?
   A this
   B that
   C these
   D they

3. For hundreds and thousands of years, people _____ plants as sources for medicines.
   A have used
   B are using
   C will use
   D use

4. _____, people on the island of Madagascar have traditionally used the rosy periwinkle for various health problems.
   A Such as
   B Including
   C Is like
   D For example

5. Today, doctors use a medicine from the rosy periwinkle to treat serious diseases _____ cancer.
   A for example
   B such as
   C for instance
   D is like

6. This "new" medicine _____ the rate of survival from cancer.
   A increasing
   B increase
   C has increased
   D have increased

B **Edit.** Re-read your draft from Step 3. Look at the editing checklist. Edit your writing.

C **Peer Edit.** Exchange drafts with a partner. Tell your partner what you like about the draft. Look at the editing checklist. Tell your partner how to improve the draft.

✓ **Editing Checklist**

me	my partner	
☐	☐	used linking verbs correctly
☐	☐	used the present perfect tense correctly
☐	☐	used demonstrative adjectives correctly
☐	☐	used signal words correctly

STEP 5 Publish

Rewrite your general-to-specific essay in your best handwriting or use a computer. Look at Kenzo's essay on page 79 for ideas. Present your general-to-specific essay to the class.

TECHNOLOGY

Using the Internet to Research Examples

- Go to an online search engine.

- Do a **keyword search** for the specific examples you are using in your essay. If they are two-word terms, then try typing them in quotation marks.

- Before clicking on the Web sites you found, evaluate the source. Is it reliable? Remember that *.gov* and most museum sites are reliable. Many *.edu* and *.net* sites may also be reliable. If you are unsure about the site, go to the page and find the "about us" link. Read how the site is created and monitored.

- Record details about your specific examples to be used in your essay.

Unit 6

Compare and Contrast

UNIT OBJECTIVES

Writing
compare and contrast essay

Organization
compare and contrast

Writing Strategies
compare and contrast words

Writing Conventions
charts and graphs

Vocabulary
music words

Grammar
passive voice
present perfect tense

Technology
using a computer to make
charts and graphs

Rock musician

Blues musician playing the slide guitar

Jump blues musicians

Punk rock musician

 Analyze Photos. Look at the photographs on this page and on page 86. Answer the questions with a partner.

1. What musical instruments do you see?

2. Have you ever heard the kind of music the people in the photographs play? What did you think of it?

3. How are the photographs related to each other?

Read. Read the compare and contrast essay about popular music.

The Influences and Variations of Blues and Rock Music

Blues and rock are two forms of popular music that have many influences and variations. Although these forms of music are hard to define, musicians and historians generally agree that blues is music with set forms and usually sad themes, while rock is music with a vocal melody accompanied by guitar, drums, and bass. Although blues and rock share many of the same influences and overlap to form new variations together, they are very different forms of music.

Blues is most heavily influenced by the call-and-response music that enslaved people sang in the fields of the southern United States while they worked. This form of singing a line and then repeating it is common in West Africa and was brought from there to the United States by enslaved African people. They were sometimes allowed to make stringed instruments like banjos and guitars to accompany their call-and response-music. In the late 1800s when they were freed, African Americans began to develop, perform, and record blues music.

The variations that came from early blues are numerous and still changing today. Early blues was very similar to country music. Record companies and radio stations called African American music of this kind *blues*, and its Caucasian counterpart was called *country*. As many African Americans moved away from farms to cities, blues developed into rural blues and urban blues. Rural blues performers often used unusual instruments like the slide guitar, which was made by sliding a knife blade or a sawed-off neck of a bottle along the strings. Unlike most rural blues, urban blues was lively music. By the 1920s and 1930s, urban blues was so lively it became known as boogie-woogie. In the 1940s, blues artists were influenced by big band swing music and added instruments such as saxophones and trumpets. This variation was known as jump blues. In the 1950s, electric instruments were added to blues and the variation electric blues was born. It is this form of blues that has most influenced rock music.

Like blues, rock developed from other forms of music, most notably blues. Rock was originally called rock and roll. Rock and roll began in the 1950s in the United States. African American artists first played rock and roll for mostly all African American audiences. Then Caucasian artists began to cover, or copy, African American artists' songs and play them for mostly Caucasian audiences.

In the same way blues varied by race and region, rock varied by race. However, it also varied by time and social or technological developments. In the 1960s, surf, folk, and psychedelic rock came out of musicians' different backgrounds and interests. Then in the 1970s, heavy metal and punk rock developed as musicians tried to reach back to the roots of blues. Soft rock developed as a variation against these louder forms.

Whereas blues has different influences and variations, rock has dozens of variations and almost as many influences. Similar to blues, which is most popular in the United States, United Kingdom, and Europe, rock has been adopted and varied by artists around the world, who in turn have added their own influence and instruments to make new variations. Whether it's blues or rock, music is an international, ever-changing art form.

Sources:
Goertzen, Valerie Woodring. "Blues." <u>World Book Encyclopedia</u>. Chicago: World Book, Inc., 2006.
McKeen, William. "Rock Music." <u>World Book Encyclopedia</u>. Chicago: World Book, Inc., 2006.

VOCABULARY

A Find each word in the reading on page 88. Look at the words around it to guess the meaning. Compare your answers with a partner.

Adjectives		Nouns		Verbs	
popular	vocal	forms	melody	accompany	influence
rural	record	influences	themes	perform	
stringed		instruments	variation	record	
urban		line		form	

B Match the word with its definition. Write the letter of the definitions next to the words.

1. accompany ___e___   **a.** sentence from a song

2. form _____   **b.** from the city

3. influence _____   **c.** from the country

4. instrument _____   **d.** an object that makes music

5. line _____   ~~**e.** to play music with someone who is playing music or singing; to play along~~

6. melody _____   **f.** the tune or notes of a song

7. record _____   **g.** to affect

8. rural _____   **h.** a kind or type

9. urban _____   **i.** of the voice

10. vocal _____   **j.** to save music on a disc so that it can be played later

C Complete these sentences using the vocabulary words from the box. Use the appropriate form of the word.

1. Boogie-woogie and jump blues are _____variations_____ of blues.

2. The _____ of this blues song is sadness.

3. Many musicians are nervous when they _____ before a large audience.

4. Surf music became _____ in the 1960s, when the sport itself became a hit.

5. The piano is actually a _____ instrument even though it doesn't look a lot like its brothers, the guitar and banjo.

6. My friend asked me to _____ her on the guitar while she sings in the talent show.

7. What _____ of music do you like best?

8. The banjo is an interesting _____, because it is both stringed like a guitar and percussive like a drum.

Passive Voice vs. Active Voice	
Active Voice Sentence	**Passive Voice Sentence**
Call-and-response music **influences** blues.	Blues **is influenced** by call-and-response music.
Performers **made** the slide guitar by sliding a knife blade or a sawed-off neck of a bottle along the strings.	The slide guitar **was made** by sliding a knife blade or a sawed-off neck of a bottle along the strings.

In passive voice the subject of the sentence receives the action. The verb phrase in passive voice is a form of _be_ + a past participle. _Blues_ (subject) _is influenced_ (passive verb).

If the doer of the action, or actor, is named, it appears in a phrase with *by*: *by call-and-response music.*

Often active voice is a better choice than passive voice. But passive voice is used in the following cases:

• when the subject is more important than the actor. (For example, *Blues* is the subject of the sentence and also the subject of the paragraph, so it's better to use passive voice to keep *Blues* at the beginning of the sentence and paragraph.)

• when the actor is understood or unknown. (For example, it is understood that rural blues performers made slide guitars because that was said in the beginning of the sentence. It is better to use passive voice to avoid repetition.)

A Change the sentences below from active voice to passive voice. Write the new sentence on the line. Not every passive voice sentence will contain a phrase with *by*.

1. Enslaved African people brought call-and-response music to the United States.
   Call-and-response music was brought to the United States by enslaved African people.

2. Their owners allowed enslaved people to make instruments.
   _____

3. In the late 1800s, the U.S. government freed enslaved African Americans.
   _____

4. People knew lively urban blues as boogie-woogie.
   _____

5. Big band swing music influenced blues artists.
   _____

6. People called this variation jump blues.
   _____

Present Perfect Tense

Active Voice	Passive Voice
Electric blues **has influenced** rock music.	Rock **has been adopted** by artists around the world.
Musicians **have made** history.	Rock and blues **have been influenced** by each other.

As we learned in Unit 5, the present perfect tense shows an action that began in the past and continues in the present or is completed in the present.

The present perfect is formed by *has* or *have* + past participle.

Present perfect can be in the active or passive voice.

The passive voice of the present perfect is formed by *has* or *have* + *been* + past participle.

B Complete the sentences using the present perfect tense of a verb from the box.

grow   ~~develop~~   call   invent   originate   use

1. Blues music ___*has developed*___ from call-and-response music.

2. Rural blues musicians _____ interesting instruments like the slide guitar.

3. Rock music _____ from blues, R&B, and jazz.

4. Some kinds of rock music _____ out of other forms of rock, like heavy metal out of hard rock.

5. Musicians from around the world _____ their country's instruments, melodies, and rhythms to influence rock.

6. That is why people _____ rock an international music.

ORGANIZATION

Compare and Contrast Essay

Remember!
A compare and contrast essay compares two or more subjects. The subjects are defined in the introduction paragraph. There are two main forms of the compare and contrast essay: the block format and the point-by-point format.

	Block Format	Point-by-Point Format
Introduction	Introduces and defines the subjects being compared.	
Middle Paragraph	Describe the features of the first subject.	Describe one point about both subjects.
Middle Paragraph	Describe the features of the second subject.	Describe another point about both subjects.
Middle Paragraph	(The above two middle paragraphs can be one or more paragraphs long.)	Describe another point about both subjects.
Conclusion	Summarizes the subjects and how they compare and contrast.	

A Complete the outline below with information from the reading on page 88.

The Influences and Variations of Blues and Rock Music

  I. Introduction

   A. Two subjects: **1.** *blues and rock; influences and variations of each*

   B. Definitions: **2.** _____

  II. Describe Blues

   A. Influences:

   3. _____

   B. Variations

   4. _____

   5. _____

   6. _____

   7. _____

   8. _____

  III. Describe Rock

   A. Influences:

   9. _____

   B. Variations

   10. _____

   11. _____

   12. _____

   13. _____

   14. _____

   15. _____

  IV. Conclusion

   A. Summary: **16.** _____

   B. Compare and Contrast: **17.** _____

B Reread the article on page 88. Answer the following questions in complete sentences.

1. Which format does the writer use, block or point-by-point?

The writer uses block format.

2. How do you know?

_____

3. How many body paragraphs are there?

_____

4. What points does the author compare and contrast?

_____

Compare and Contrast Words

> **Remember!**
> Words that signal **comparison** are: *similarly, just like, likewise, in the same way, just as, in comparison.* Words that signal **contrast** are: *in contrast, however, but, on the other hand, whereas, yet.*

Find compare and contrast words. Find the following expressions in the reading on page 88. Copy the sentence that contains the word or phrase.

1. Like: *Like blues, rock developed from other forms of music, most notably blues.*

2. However: _____

3. Whereas: _____

4. Similar to: _____

WRITING CONVENTIONS

Charts and Graphs

> **Remember!**
> **Charts and graphs** give information visually. You can include charts or graphs to give more information, explain important or complex information, or compare and contrast information from your essay.

OFFICIAL SURVEY SONGS OF THE WEEK

PHOENIX, ARIZONA . . . . APRIL 16, 1960

NO.	RECORD	ARTIST	LABEL
1.	GREENFIELDS	BROTHERS FOUR	COLUMBIA
2.	FOOTSTEPS	STEVE LAWRENCE	ABC
3.	FANNY MAE	BUSTER BROWN	FIRE
4.	LET THE LITTLE GIRL DANCE	BILY BLAND	OLD TOWN
5.	ONLY IN MI DREAMS	FRANK FAFARA	MCI

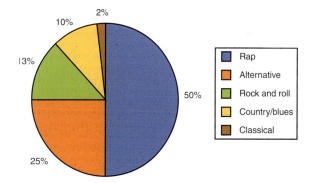

Pie chart: Rap 50%, Alternative 25%, Rock and roll 13%, Country/blues 10%, Classical 2%

Discuss these questions about each chart or graph with a partner.

1. What is the name of the chart or graph? Why do you think it is named that?

2. What does the chart or graph show?

3. What can you learn from this chart or graph?

4. What kinds of information can you record in this kind of chart or graph?

Compare and Contrast Essay

A **compare and contrast essay** is a nonfiction text, usually five or more paragraphs long. This kind of essay compares, or tells the similarities, and contrasts, or tells the differences, between two or more subjects. The introduction paragraph defines or explains the two subjects. It also gives a thesis, or main idea, statement that tells what points will be compared and contrasted about the subjects. Then each body paragraph explains either one subject or one point about both subjects. Compare and contrast essays are often found in magazine or newspaper articles and textbooks.

 A **Read.** Read Carmine's essay comparing Italian and Indian foods.

Indian and Italian Food Friends

by Carmine Giovino

My best friend is Indian, and I am Italian. Every weekend we eat dinner together. You might think that we have very different tastes in food. However, we have found that although Indian and Italian meals use very different seasoning, they include many of the same ingredients and a mix of similar and different food preparation methods.

Both Italian and Indian foods include many seasonings. Typical Italian seasoning comes from herbs, or dried plant leaves. The most common Italian herbs include basil, oregano, parsley, and rosemary. These herbs are mild but each has a distinct taste. Some Italian cooks occasionally use stronger spices like cinnamon, which is a sweet spice made from tree bark and used in American desserts, or paprika, which is a spicy Eastern European pepper. My father adds cinnamon to the cheese mixture he puts in pasta. However, sweet and strong spices are not common in most Italian food. Indian seasoning, on the other hand, is generally strong, and sweet or spicy. Indian cooks use spices, or ground up bark, roots, and seeds. The most common Indian spices are curry, cardamom, cumin, chili peppers, and turmeric. My best friend's mother uses all of these spices in one meal!

Seasoning is the biggest difference between Italian and Indian cooking. However, the ingredients are often very similar. Tomatoes are very important to Italian foods. Sauces made from tomatoes are part of many meals. Similarly, many Indian sauces include tomatoes. Likewise, rice and wheat are important ingredients in meals of both cultures. Italian cooks make famous rice dishes called risotto. In the same way, many Indian meals includes rice. Wheat is essential to Italian pasta, breads, and pizzas, just as it is to Indian breads. Italian cooks use peas, eggplant, potatoes, spinach, chicken, and lamb as important parts of the meal just like most Indian cooks do. These ingredients have been used by both Indian and Italian cooks for centuries.

Food preparation, or how these spices and ingredients are cooked, has some similarities and differences between the two cultures. Both Indian and Italian cooks simmer, or slowly cook, their sauces. They mix together tomatoes, spices, meats, and other vegetables. Then they let them cook for hours. This makes the sauces thick and tasty. Although sauce preparation is similar, bread making can vary. Italian cooks bake their loaves of breads in ovens. Yeast is included, so the bread is often light and fluffy. Indian cooks sometimes bake their breads, but do not use yeast, so they are often flat and dense. Sometimes Indian

---

cooks fry their breads in hot oil. This method makes light, puffy breads. No matter how they make the breads, Indians and Italians love to dip them into their thick, rich sauces.

So whether we're learning to cook from his Indian mother or my Italian father, or we're going to our favorite restaurants, my best friend and I enjoy the same ingredients prepared with very different methods and spices. I'm learning to like spicy, boldly seasoned foods. My best friend is learning to appreciate more subtle or mild meals. Sometimes we even try combining Italian herbs and Indian spices in a sauce we serve over pasta! Whatever we eat for a meal, we can always agree on the dessert—American ice cream!

B **Summarize.** Re-read Carmine's essay about Italian and Indian food on page 94. Summarize each paragraph below the correct picture. The first one has been done for you.

I.

My best friend is Indian. I am Italian. We eat dinner together every weekend. You might think we have different tastes, but we have found that although seasoning differs, ingredients do not.

II.

_____

_____

III.

_____

_____

Purpose: Compare and Contrast Two Subjects

WRITING PROMPT

Write a five-paragraph essay comparing and contrasting two subjects. Share the essay with your teacher and classmates.

✓ Prompt Checklist

- ❑ I read the task carefully.
- ❑ I understood the form, audience, topic, and purpose of the prompt.

STEP 1 Pre-write

A Look at Carmine's list of possible subjects and points to compare and contrast. Make your own list. You might want to list social customs from your culture and another culture. Or you could make a list of hobbies, activities, or events.

Carmine's List of Subjects

two foods	schools in my parents' country and here
my best friend's Indian meals and my Italian meals	my two favorite movies
two sports	my favorite book and my least favorite book
two after-school clubs	

B After you have chosen two subjects, list all the points that you can compare and contrast between them. You may want to use a chart like Carmine's.

Carmine's Chart

Indian and Italian Food		
Indian Food	**Same**	**Italian Food**
sweet, strong spices: curry, cardamom, turmeric, cumin, chili pepper	Ingredients: tomatoes, rice, wheat, peas, eggplant, spinach, chicken, lamb	Herbs: basil, oregano, rosemary, parsley
Fry their breads; no yeast, flat breads	Simmer their sauces	Yeast breads: light and fluffy

Look at Carmine's outline. Make your own outline about the subjects you chose.

Carmine's Outline

Title: Indian and Italian Food Friends

I. Introduction

    A. My best friend and I: our friendship, our backgrounds, our food

    B. Thesis Statement: We've found that although Indian and Italian meals use very different seasoning, they include many of the same ingredients and a mix of similar and different food preparation methods.

II. Body 1

    A. Italian herbs

        1. What are they: dried plant leaves: oregano, basil, parsley, rosemary

        2. Other spices: paprika, and cinnamon like in father's cheese mixture

    B. Indian spices

        1. Strong and sweet: curry, cardamom, cumin, tumeric, chili peppers

        2. Best friend's mother uses them all in one sauce.

III. Body 2

    A. Similar ingredients

        1. Tomatoes, rice, wheat, peas, eggplant, potatoes, spinach, chicken, and lamb

IV. Body 3

    A. Food preparation.

        1. Sauces are similar: they simmer.

        2. Breads are different: Italian uses yeast, so they're light and fluffy. Indian are flat or they fry it to make it puffy.

V. Conclusion

    A. We cook together.

        1. We've tried mixing the spices and herbs over pasta.

        2. We agree on ice cream!

STEP 3 Draft and Revise

 Practice. Look at Carmine's first draft. How can he improve it? Answer the questions.

First Draft
Indian and Italian Food Friends
by Carmine Giovino

(1) My best friend is Indian, and I am Italian. (2) Every weekend we eat dinner together. (3) You might think that we have very different tastes in food. (4) However, we think that although Indian and Italian meals use very different seasoning, they include many of the same ingredients, and a mix of similar and different food preparation methods.

(5) Both Italian and Indian foods include many seasonings. (6) Typical Italian seasoning comes from herbs, or dried plant leaves. (7) The most common Italian herbs include basil, oregano, parsley, and rosemary. (8) These herbs are mild but each has a distinct taste. (9) Some Italian cooks occasionally use stronger spices like cinnamon, which is a sweet spice made from tree bark and used in American desserts, or paprika, which is a spicy Eastern European pepper. (10) My father adds cinnamon to the cheese mixture he puts in pasta. (11) However, sweet and strong spices are not common in most Italian food. (12) Indian seasoning, on the other hand, is generally strong and sweet or spicy. (13) Indian cooks use spices or ground up bark, roots, and seeds. (14) The most common Indian spices are curry, cardamom, cumin, chili peppers, and turmeric. (15) My best friend's mother uses all of these spices in one meal!

(16) Seasoning is the biggest difference between Italian and Indian cooking. (17) However, the ingredients are often very similar. (18) Tomatoes are very important to Italian foods. (19) Sauces made from tomatoes are part of many meals. (20) Many Indian sauces include tomatoes. (21) Rice and wheat are important ingredients in meals of both cultures. (22) Italian cooks make famous rice dishes called risotto. (23) In the same way, many Indian meals includes rice. (24) Wheat is essential to Italian pasta, breads, and pizzas, just as it is to Indian breads. (25) Italian cooks use peas, eggplant, potatoes, spinach, chicken, and lamb as important parts of the meal just like most Indian cooks do.

(26) Food preparation or how these spices and ingredients are cooked has some similarities and differences between the two cultures. (27) Both Indian and Italian cooks simmer, or slowly cook, their sauces. (28) They mix together tomatoes, spices, meats, and other vegetables. (29) Then they let them cook for hours. (30) This makes the sauces thick and tasty. (31) Although sauce preparation is similar, bread making can vary. (32) Italian

cooks bake their loaves of breads in ovens. (33) They include yeast, so the bread is often light and fluffy. (34) Indian cooks sometimes bake their breads, but do not use yeast, so they are often flat and dense. (35) Sometimes Indian cooks fry their breads in hot oil. (36) This method makes light, puffy breads. (37) No matter how they make the breads, Indians and Italians love to dip them into their thick, rich sauces.

(38) So whether we're learning to cook from his Indian mother or my Italian father, or we're going to our favorite restaurants, my best friend and I enjoy the same ingredients prepared with very different methods and spices. (38) I'm learning to like spicy, boldly seasoned foods. (39) My best friend is learning to appreciate more subtle or mild meals. (40) Sometimes we even try combining Italian herbs and Indian spices in a sauce we serve over pasta! (41) Whatever we eat for a meal, we can always agree on the dessert—American ice cream!

1. How can Carmine BEST rewrite sentence 4?
   A Change *think* to *have find*.
   B Change *think* to *are finding*.
   C Change *think* to *have found*.
   D Change *think* to *are found*.

2. Which word or phrase can Carmine add to the beginning of sentence 20?
   A Similarly,
   B Just like
   C Yet,
   D However,

3. Which word or phrase can Carmine add to the beginning of sentence 21?
   A Yet,
   B Likewise,
   C On the other hand,
   D Whereas

4. What sentence can Carmine add after sentence 25?
   A These ingredients have been used by both Indian and Italian cooks for centuries.
   B These ingredients are used by both Indian and Italian cooks for centuries.
   C These ingredients have used by both Indian and Italian cooks for centuries.
   D These ingredients are being used by both Indian and Italian cooks for centuries.

5. What would be the best illustration for paragraph 3?
   A a chart of Italian herbs
   B a chart of Indian spices
   C a pie graph of Italian and Indian cooks in the world
   D a chart of Italian and Indian ingredients

6. How can Carmine best rewrite sentence 33 to be in the passive voice?
   A Change *They include yeast* to *Yeast is included*
   B Change *They include yeast* to *Yeast was included*
   C Change *They include yeast* to *Yeast is including*
   D Change *They include yeast* to *They have included yeast*

B **Draft.** Write a first draft of your compare and contrast essay. Use your notes from Steps 1 and 2.

C **Revise.** Read your first draft. How can you improve it? Look at the revision checklist. Revise your writing.

STEP 4 Edit

A **Practice.** Look at the sentences. Choose the best substitute for the underlined words. If the sentence is correct, choose "Make no change."

1. Writing and singing may seem like very different activities initially, but I <u>have find</u> they have many similarities.
   A have finding
   Ⓑ have found
   C am found
   D Make no change.

2. Singing uses a <u>stringed</u> instrument.
   A popular
   B vocal
   C accompanied
   D Make no change.

3. <u>Just like</u> writing uses a pen.
   A Similarly,
   B But
   C Whereas
   D Make no change.

4. However, they are both <u>instruments</u>, or tools, for the activity.
   A melodies
   B variations
   C influences
   D Make no change.

5. I find singing relaxing. <u>In contrast</u>, I feel at ease when I am writing.
   A In the same way,
   B Yet
   C However,
   D Make no change.

6. Songs <u>are singing</u> by people all over the world,
   A are sing
   B sing
   C are sung
   D Make no change.

7. Just as words <u>are written</u> by people all over the world.
   A are writing
   B are wrote
   C have written
   D Make no change.

8. I <u>have singing</u> many songs and written many stories. Now, I think I will write some songs.
   A have sing
   B have sung
   C am sung
   D Make no change.

B **Edit.** Re-read your draft from Step 3. Look at the editing checklist. Edit your writing.

C **Peer Edit.** Exchange drafts with a partner. Tell your partner what you like about the draft. Look at the editing checklist. Tell your partner how to improve the draft.

Editing Checklist

me	my partner	
❏	❏	used passive voice correctly
❏	❏	used the present perfect tense correctly
❏	❏	used compare and contrast signal words correctly
❏	❏	used vocabulary correctly

STEP 5 Publish

Rewrite your compare and contrast essay in your best handwriting or use a computer. Look at Carmine's essay on page 94 for ideas. Add a photograph or drawing if you want. Present your compare and contrast essay to the class.

TECHNOLOGY

Using a Computer to Make Charts and Graphs

- Open your presentation or word processing software.
- Find the templates for charts or graphs.
- Review the different chart and graph formats. Choose the best one for your essay.
- Record the information from your essay or source in the chart or graph.
- Label all important parts of the chart or graph.

GROUP WRITING

Work in a group to write about one of these topics. Follow the steps below.

1. Choose your topic.
2. Discuss and record information.
3. Do research if you need to.
4. Write a first draft.
5. Revise and edit the draft with your group.
6. Present your group's essay to the class.

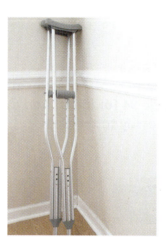

Topic 1

Write a general-to-specific, five-paragraph essay about a health topic that concerns you. Write about the general topic, then give specific examples.

Topic 2

Write a compare and contrast essay about two things, such as two different kinds of music or two different kinds of food.

TIMED WRITING

Choose one writing prompt. Complete the writing task in 45 minutes.

WRITING PROMPT 1

Write a five-paragraph general-to-specific essay about modern technological devices. Choose devices that have a common purpose. Choose objects that you understand and can explain.

WRITING PROMPT 2

Write a five-paragraph compare and contrast essay about two different kinds of transportation. Describe each kind of transportation and how it works. Tell the benefits and drawbacks of each.

 Test Tip

Thesis Statement! Remember to end your introduction paragraph with a thesis statement that tells the points your essay covers.

SELF-CHECK

Think about your writing skills. Check (✔) the answers that are true.

1. I understand. . .
   - ❏ health words.
   - ❏ music words.

2. I can correctly. . .
   - ❏ draw conclusions.
   - ❏ use words that signal example.
   - ❏ use compare and contrast words.

3. I can. . .
   - ❏ use present perfect tense.
   - ❏ use linking verbs.
   - ❏ use demonstrative adjectives and pronouns.
   - ❏ use passive voice.

4. I can correctly. . .
   - ❏ paraphrase information.
   - ❏ make charts and graphs.

5. I can organize my writing. . .
   - ❏ from general to specific.
   - ❏ point by point.
   - ❏ subject by subject.

6. I can write to. . .
   - ❏ generalize information.
   - ❏ compare and contrast.

Unit 7

Response to Literature

UNIT OBJECTIVES

Writing
response to literature

Organization
five-paragraph essay with
   three-part thesis statement

Writing Strategies
combining information with
   relative clauses
connecting ideas with transition
   words

Writing Conventions
summarizing

Vocabulary
literary analysis words

Grammar
past perfect tense

Technology
using a computer to research
   an author

Migrant worker boys

Migrant worker

Island in the Pacific Ocean

  A **Analyze Photos.** Look at the photographs on this page and on page 104. Complete the following activities with a partner.

1. Describe each photograph in detail. What do you see? Use strong verbs, nouns, and adjectives.

2. Imagine you are in each place. What would you be doing? How would you feel? Why would feel that way?

Read. Read the response to literature essay about the short story "The Circuit" by Francisco Jiménez.

Powerful Imagery and Symbols in "The Circuit"

Francisco Jiménez writes autobiographical short stories. In them, he describes his childhood as a migrant worker in Mexico and California. In the story "The Circuit," Ponchito, who is a sixth-grade boy, tells the story of his life as a migrant worker. Ponchito and his family move to a new farm each season. As a result, Ponchito goes to school only when he is not working. Jiménez vividly shows that Ponchito's life is difficult, but rich. He describes Ponchito's family, environment, and emotions with imagery, or powerful pictures, and symbols.

To help describe Ponchito's parents, Jimenez uses symbols. Papá's car and Mamá's pot represent more than just a vehicle and a household item. They show their owners' personalities. Jiménez tells how Papá had bought the car. "He checked it thoroughly before driving it out of the car lot. He examined every inch of the car. He listened to the motor" (75). The car shows that Papá is a careful, proud man. In the same way, Mamá's pot highlights her personality. "It was an old large galvanized pot she had picked up at an army surplus store in Santa Maria. The pot had many dents and nicks, and the more dents and nicks it acquired the more Mamá liked it" (76). The pot is old and dented. Nevertheless, it is large and useful. Mamá is proud of her pot. In the symbol of the pot, we learn that Mamá is sensible and adaptable.

Jiménez uses personification and other imagery techniques to describe Ponchito's environment. In other words, to describe the mountains and the sunset, Jiménez writes that they are like people. "Finally the mountains around the valley reached out and swallowed the sun" (79). The reader has a clear image of the sunset. In the same way, Jiménez describes the vines in the vineyard. "The vines blanketed the grapes, making it difficult to see the bunches" (79). In place of saying the vines cover the grapes, Jiménez gives us an image in which they act like a person putting a blanket over them.

Jiménez chooses precise words to describe Ponchito's physical discomfort so that the reader can sympathize with him. Ponchito is picking grapes in the hot sun. With a clear image, Jiménez helps the reader see how hot and thirsty Ponchito is. Jiménez writes, "I was completely soaked in sweat, and my mouth felt as if I had been chewing on a handkerchief" (78). The reader almost feels thirsty imagining chewing on a handkerchief. Jiménez describes Ponchito's emotions similarly. Ponchito goes back to school for the first time in November, which is after the grape harvest is over. He has forgotten English and feels nervous and embarrassed about it. Jiménez does not just tell the reader Ponchito's feelings at being asked to read aloud. Instead, he uses strong words to describe them. He writes, "My mouth was dry. My eyes began to water. I could not begin"(82). The reader can see and feel how Ponchito feels.

Throughout the short story, Jiménez describes Ponchito's family, environment, and emotions in vivid detail. In fact, Jiménez creates powerful images in readers' minds through symbols, personification, and carefully chosen words. Jiménez's imagery allows the reader to truly see the hard and honest world of a migrant working family.

Source:
Jiménez, Francisco. "The Circuit." The Circuit: Stories from the Life of a Migrant Child. Albuquerque: University of New Mexico Press, 1997.

VOCABULARY

A Find each word in the reading on page 106. Look at the words around it to guess the meaning. Compare your answers with a partner's.

Adjectives	Adverb	Nouns		Verbs
adaptable	vividly	detail	symbol	describe
autobiographical		environment	technique	examine
precise		imagery		highlight
rich		personality		sympathize
vivid		personification		

B Complete the sentences with words from the box.

1. _____*Personification*_____ is to give human traits to a non-human thing.

2. In art and literature, the use of language to appeal to one's senses and to create a mental picture is _____.

3. Something that represents something else is a _____.

4. _____ give more information about a topic or idea.

5. A person's qualities, such as their traits, habits, moods, and attitudes, make up his or her _____.

6. When something is very easy or clear to see or imagine, it is _____.

C Answer these questions using words from the box in Activity A.

1. What do you call a story that is written by and about a person? ____*autobiographical*____

2. What is another word for *surroundings*? _____

3. What word means both *full of money* and *full of detail*? _____

4. What is another word for *methods*? _____

5. When an author emphasizes something, he or she does what? _____

6. What do you call something that is exact? _____

7. What is the word for what a reader does to look closely at a text? _____

8. When a reader feels what a character feels, he or she does what? _____

Simple Past	Past Perfect
Jimenéz tells how Papa **bought** the car.	Jimenéz tells how Papa **had bought** the car.
It was an old large galvanized pot she **picked** up at an army surplus store.	It was an old large galvanized pot she **had picked** up at an army surplus store.

The past perfect is used to talk about actions that happened before something else happened in the past.

To form the past perfect, use: *had* (simple past of *have*) + past participle of the verb.

Change the verb in bold to the past perfect tense and rewrite the sentence.

1. Jimenéz **lived** most of these experiences before writing about them.

   Jimenéz had lived most of these experiences before writing about them.

2. People **heard** very little about migrant's lives when Jimenéz started writing.

   _____

3. Papa **listened** to the car before he bought it.

   _____

4. Jimenéz **described** what Mama's pot looked like by the time she got into the car with it.

   _____

5. Ponchito **spoke** Spanish before he learned English in school.

   _____

6. Ponchito **worked** in the fields only a little by the time the story begins.

   _____

7. By the end of the story, Ponchito **became** comfortable at school.

   _____

8. He **felt** happy before he found out he was moving again.

   _____

Five-Paragraph Essay with Three-Part Thesis

Complete the outline below with information from the reading on page 106.

> **Remember!**
> A **five-paragraph essay** has an introduction paragraph, three body paragraphs, and a conclusion paragraph. At the end of the introduction paragraph is the thesis statement, or sentence that gives the main points of the essay. Often in five-paragraph essays, **the thesis statement has three parts**, or three main points. Then each body paragraph discusses one of the three points.

Powerful Imagery and Symbols in "The Circuit"

I. Introduction

    A. Introduce the title and author: **1.** _Francisco Jiménez writes autobiographical short stories. In them, he describes his childhood as a migrant worker in Mexico and California._

    B. Brief summary of the story: **2.** _____

    _____

    C. Three-part thesis statement: **3.** _____

    _____

II. Body Paragraph I

    A. Main point: **4.** _____

    _____

      1. Evidence for/example of the main point: **5.** _____

    _____

      2. **6.** _____

    _____

III. Body Paragraph II

    A. Main point: **7.** _____

    _____

      1. Evidence for/example of the main point: **8.** _____

    _____

      2. **9.** _____

IV. Body Paragraph III

    A. Main point: **10.** _____

    _____

      1. Evidence for/example of the main point: **11.** _____

    _____

      2. **12.** _____

    _____

V. Conclusion

    A. Summary of the main points: **13.** _____

Combining Information with Relative Clauses

Write new sentences using a relative pronoun to make a relative clause.

1. He describes Ponchito's family, environment, and emotions with imagery. Imagery is powerful pictures and symbols. *He describes Ponchito's family, environment, and emotions with imagery, which is powerful pictures, and symbols.*

2. At the beginning of the story, Jimenez describes Ponchito returning to his home. Ponchito's home is a shack. _____

3. Ponchito's father checked the car thoroughly. He is always careful. _____

4. Ponchito realizes that they are moving to a new place. The new place is a vineyard. _____

5. Ponchito knows he will have to pick grapes. Picking grapes is a very hard job. _____

6. Ponchito goes back to school for the first time in November. He goes back after the grape harvest is over. _____

7. At school, Ponchito meets his teacher. His teacher becomes a friend. _____

8. Ponchito finds out he has to move again. Finding this out is very hard for him. _____

Connecting Ideas with Transition Words

Find the following phrases in the reading on page 106. Complete the chart below by writing the two ideas that the transition word connects.

Find the following phrases in the reading on page 106.

Remember!
The following words and phrases are used to connect ideas between sentences. Each word or phrase shows a certain relationship between the two pieces of information.

As a result, (result/effect)
In fact, (emphasis)
In other words, (repetition)
Instead, (alternative)
Nevertheless, (contrast)

These words and phrases usually come at the beginning of the sentence and are always followed by a comma.

Transition Word	Ideas Connected
1. As a result,	*Ponchito's family moves to a new farm each season.* *Ponchito goes to school only when he's not working.*
2. Nevertheless,	
3. In other words,	
4. Instead,	
5. In fact,	

WRITING CONVENTIONS

Summarizing

Remember!
When you write **response to literature** essays, you summarize all or part of the text you are writing about. **Summaries** are short, clear statements telling the main ideas of a text.

Reread the essay on page 106. Summarize each section in two to three sentences.

Reread the essay on page 106.

1. The whole short story: *In the story "The Circuit," a sixth-grade boy named Ponchito tells the story of his life as a migrant worker. Ponchito and his family move to a new farm each season. As a result, Ponchito goes to school only when he is not working.*

2. Ponchito's family: _____

   _____

   _____

3. Ponchito's environment: _____

   _____

   _____

4. Ponchito's experience at school: _____

   _____

   _____

Response to Literature Essay

A **response to literature essay** is a nonfiction text, usually five or more paragraphs long. This kind of essay tells what the writer thinks about another text. The introduction paragraph introduces the literature and the author. Next is a brief summary of the text. The essay also gives a thesis statement that tells what points the writer is discussing about the text. Then each body paragraph explains a point in the thesis and gives examples from the text. Response to literature essays are often found in magazine articles and textbooks.

  A **Read.** Read Javier's response to Scott O'Dell's novel *The Island of the Blue Dolphins*.

The Island of the Blue Dolphins

by Javier Lopez

True stories can inspire and teach people. Scott O'Dell, in his novel *The Island of the Blue Dolphins*, tells the true story of Karana. She was a young girl who lived for many years alone on a deserted island. In the beginning of the novel, O'Dell captures the reader's attention with his intriguing setting and plot. Then throughout the story, he teaches the reader about the themes of strength and determination through Karana's character.

The setting of *The Island of the Blue Dolphins*, as the title indicates, is an island in the Pacific Ocean. At the beginning of the novel, the island had been inhabited by a small tribe of people. However, explorers in ships come to take the people off the island, supposedly to give them a better life. So throughout the novel, the island is deserted except for Karana and, in the first part of the story, her brother. The island is small but has rich plant and animal life. There are grasses, short trees, and sea plants. Foxes, wild dogs, seals, and other ocean animals inhabit the island and the surrounding waters. The landscape varies from beach to rocky cliffs. This rich and varied setting captures the reader's attention from the beginning.

O'Dell maintains the reader's interest and enthusiasm through the exciting plot. The story begins with the arrival of explorers in ships. Then suddenly the village is packing up to leave the island. As if this were not dramatic enough, something unexpected happens as the villagers are leaving. Karana, who is one of the young girls from the village, notices that her brother is not with them. He is still on the island. Karana refuses to leave her brother behind. She jumps off the ship and swims back to him. Now they are both stranded on the newly deserted island. The plot continues at this same exciting pace throughout the novel. O'Dell tells the adventures of Karana through one thrilling event after another.

Throughout the story, we learn about important themes O'Dell wishes to teach: strength and determination. Karana has incredible internal strength. She gives up the chance to be with her family and village to save her brother. In the middle of the story, Karana's brother is killed by wild dogs. Karana is very sad. She mourns the loss of her brother. Nevertheless, she is determined to survive. She lives on without him, which takes incredible inner strength. Karana also shows physical strength during her time on the island. She fights wild animals to protect herself. She gathers food, catches animals, and builds a shelter. In other words, she survives alone on the island for eighteen years. Karana

---

is lonely and scared, yet she perseveres. This requires amazing strength and determination. O'Dell shows the reader how one girl can survive and thrive in very difficult situations.

Scott O'Dell once explained why he writes books for children rather than adults. He said, "The only reason I write is to say something. I've forsaken adults because they're not going to change, although they may try awfully hard. But children can and do change." O'Dell wrote *The Island of the Blue Dolphins* to show young readers how a rich and dangerous setting and a series of exciting events can make a person strong and determined.

Source: O'Dell, Scott. <u>The Island of the Blue Dolphins</u>. New York: Scholastic, 1997.

B **Summarize.** Re-read Javier's essay on *The Island of the Blue Dolphins* on page 112. Summarize each paragraph below the correct picture. The first has been done for you.

I.

Scott O'Dell tells the true story of Karana, who survived for many years on a deserted island. The reader is intrigued and taught by O'Dell's story.

III.

_____

_____

_____

_____

II.

_____

_____

_____

_____

IV.

_____

_____

_____

_____

V.

_____

_____

_____

_____

STEP-BY-STEP WRITING

Purpose: Respond to Literature

WRITING PROMPT

Write a five-paragraph essay in response to a short story or novel you have read. Share the essay with your teacher and classmates.

STEP 1 Pre-write

A Look at Javier's web of possible points to discuss. Make your own web.

Javier's Web

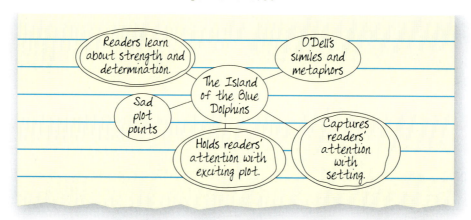

B After you have decided which points to include in your essay, reread the short story or skim the novel to find examples of these points. Create a chart like Javier's.

Javier's Chart

The Island of the Blue Dolphins		
Captures readers' attention with the setting.	Holds readers' attention with exciting plot.	Readers learn about strength and determination.
Environment: trees, rocks, beaches, etc.	Beginning: ships arrive, people leave, Karana sees her brother, she jumps off ship.	Karana's inner strength to leave the villagers to be with her brother, then to continue on after his death.
Animals: wild dogs, foxes, seals, dolphins, etc.	Middle: Karana's brother dies, Karana builds shelter.	Karana's physical strength to survive for eighteen years on an island alone: building shelter, finding food, etc.

STEP 2 Organize

Look at Javier's outline. Make your own outline about the text you chose.

Javier's Outline

Title: The Island of the Blue Dolphins

I. Introduction

  A. True stories teach us: *The Island of the Blue Dolphins* by Scott O'Dell is true.

  B. Summary of the story: Karana lives on a deserted island for a long time.

  C. Thesis: In the beginning of the novel, O'Dell captures the reader's attention with his intriguing setting and plot. Then throughout the story, he teaches the reader about the themes of strength and determination through Karana's character.

II. Body 1 Captures the reader's attention with setting:

  A. Environment: trees, rocks, beaches, etc.

  B. Animals: wild dogs, foxes, seals, dolphins, etc.

III. Body 2 Keeps reader's attention with plot:

  A. Beginning: ships arrive, people leave, Karana sees her brother, she jumps off ship.

  B. Middle: Karana's brother dies, she builds shelter.

IV. Body 3 Teaches reader about strength and determination

  A. Karana's inner strength to leave the villagers to be with her brother then to continue on after his death.

  B. Karana's physical strength to survive for eighteen years on an island alone: building shelter, finding food, etc.

V. Conclusion

  A. Scott O'Dell writes for young people because he wants to teach them.

STEP 3 Draft and Revise

A **Practice.** Look at Javier's first draft. How can he improve it? Answer the questions.

First Draft

The Island of the Blue Dolphins

by Javier Lopez

(1) True stories can inspire and teach people. (2) Scott O'Dell, in his novel *The Island of the Blue Dolphins,* tells the true story of Karana. (3) In the beginning of the novel, O'Dell captures the reader's attention with his intriguing setting and plot. (4) Then throughout the story, he teaches the reader about the themes of strength and determination through Karana's character.

(5) The setting of *The Island of the Blue Dolphins,* as the title indicates, is an island in the Pacific Ocean. (6) At the beginning of the novel, the island had inhabited by a small tribe of people. (7) However, explorers in ships come to take the people off the island, supposedly to give them a better life. (8) So throughout the novel, the island is deserted except for Karana and, in the first part of the story, her brother. (9) The island is small but has rich plant and animal life. (10) There are grasses, short trees, and sea plants. (11) Foxes, wild dogs, seals, and other ocean animals inhabit the island and the surrounding waters. (12) The landscape varies from beach to rocky cliffs. (13) This rich and varied setting captures the reader's attention from the beginning.

(14) O'Dell maintains the reader's interest and enthusiasm through the exciting plot. (15) The story begins with the arrival of explorers in ships. (16) Then suddenly the village is packing up to leave the island. (17) As if this were not dramatic enough, something unexpected happens as the villagers are leaving. (18) Karana is one of the young girls from the village. (19) Karana notices that her brother is not with them. (20) He is still on the island. (21) Karana refuses to leave her brother behind. (22) She jumps off the ship and swims back to him. (23) Now they are both stranded on the newly deserted island. (24) The plot continues at this same exciting pace throughout the novel. (25) O'Dell tells the adventures of Karana through one thrilling event after another.

(26) Throughout the story, we learn about important themes O'Dell wishes to teach: strength and determination. (27) Karana has incredible internal strength. (28) She gives up the chance to be with her family and village to save her brother. (29) In the middle of the story, Karana's brother is killed by wild dogs. (30) Karana is very sad. (31) She mourns the loss of her brother.

---

(32) She is determined to survive. (33) She lives on without him, which takes incredible inner strength. (34) Karana also shows physical strength during her time on the island. (35) She fights wild animals to protect herself. (36) She had gathered food, catches animals, and builds a shelter. (37) She survives alone on the island for eighteen years. (38) Karana is lonely and scared, yet she perseveres. (39) This requires amazing strength and determination. (40) O'Dell shows the reader how one girl can survive and thrive in very difficult situations.

(41) Scott O'Dell once explained why he writes books for children rather than adults. (42) He said, "The only reason I write is to say something. (43) I've forsaken adults because they're not going to change, although they may try awfully hard. (44) But children can and do change." (45) O'Dell wrote *The Island of the Blue Dolphins* to show young readers how a rich and dangerous setting and a series of exciting events can make a person strong and determined.

1. What summary of the novel should Javier add after sentence 2?
   A I very much enjoyed this novel and know you would, too.
   (B) She was a young girl who lived for many years alone on a deserted island.
   C *The Island of the Blue Dolphins* by Scott O'Dell is an inspiring true story.
   D *The Island of the Blue Dolphins* reminds me of *The Cay* by Theodore Taylor.

2. How can Javier best improve sentence 6?
   A Change *had inhabited* to *had been inhabited.*
   B Change *had inhabited* to *was inhabited.*
   C Change *had inhabited* to *have inhabited.*
   D Change *had inhabited* to *are inhabited.*

3. How can Javier BEST combine sentences 18 and 19?
   A Karana who is one of the young girls from the village, she notices that her brother is not with them.
   B Karana, one of the young girls from the village, she notices that her brother is not with them.

   C Karana is one of the young girls from the village and she notices that her brother is not with them.
   D Karana, who is one of the young girls from the village, notices that her brother is not with them.

4. What word or phrase should Javier add to the beginning of sentence 32?
   A As a result,
   B In other words,
   C Nevertheless,
   D Instead,

5. How can Javier best rewrite sentence 36?
   A Change *had gathered* to *are gathering*
   B Change *had gathered* to *is gathering*
   C Change *had gathered* to *was gathering*
   D Change *had gathered* to *gathers*

6. What word or phrase should Javier add to the beginning of sentence 37?
   A In fact,
   B However,
   C Nevertheless,
   D Instead,

B **Draft.** Write a first draft of your response to literature essay. Use your notes from Steps 1 and 2.

C **Revise.** Read your first draft. How can you improve it? Look at the revision checklist. Revise your writing.

STEP 4 Edit

A **Practice.** Read the sentences. Choose the best word or phrase to complete each sentence.

1. The first person to help Robert Allen was Claudine Halpers _____.
   A who she was the county librarian
   B and the county librarian
   Ⓒ who was the county librarian
   D which is the county librarian

2. She encouraged Robert to take the GED, _____.
   A the high school equivalent test
   B which is the high school equivalent test
   C it is the high school equivalent test
   D who is the high school equivalent test

3. _____, Robert passed the GED and entered Bethel College.
   A As a result,
   B In other words,
   C Instead,
   D Nevertheless,

4. Another person who _____ Robert was a teacher at Bethel College.
   A is helping
   B were helping
   C had helped
   D will helped

5. Robert was an excellent student at Bethel College. _____ he received a scholarship to Vanderbilt University.
   A In fact,
   B Nevertheless,

C Instead,
D In other words,

6. At first, Robert's poor appearance _____ his classmates and teachers. Then they got used to it.
   A was shocking
   B had shocked
   C is shocking
   D will shock

7. Before graduating, Robert _____ about what he wanted to do. When he graduated, he knew he wanted to get a job.
   A will think
   B was thinking
   C thinks
   D had thought

8. Robert Allen was poor, but didn't let that stop him. _____ he worked hard and achieved his goals.
   A As a result,
   B Instead,
   C Nevertheless
   D In fact

B **Edit.** Re-read your draft from Step 3. Look at the editing checklist. Edit your writing.

 C **Peer Edit.** Exchange drafts with a partner. Tell your partner what you like about the draft. Look at the editing checklist. Tell your partner how to improve the draft.

Editing Checklist

me	my partner	
❏	❏	used the past perfect tense correctly
❏	❏	used transition words correctly
❏	❏	used relative clauses and commas correctly

STEP 5 Publish

Rewrite your response to literature essay in your best handwriting or use a computer. Look at Javier's essay on page 112 for ideas. Present your response to literature essay to the class.

TECHNOLOGY

Using a Computer to Research Your Author

 Find out more about the author of the short story or novel you chose.

- Use a search engine.
- Choose reliable sources.
- Read several Web sites about the author.
- Use an *image* search engine to find pictures of the author. Most search engines have an "image" button you can select in order to find images. As with a keyword search, you type in the author's name after selecting the image button. Then you hit *return* or select *search*. Look at the different images of the author. Does he or she look as you imagined? Why or why not?
- Share your discoveries with the class.

Unit 8

Technical Writing

UNIT OBJECTIVES

Writing
technical writing: process
   description

Organization
sequential essay

Writing Strategies
sequence words
using a scenario for support

Writing Conventions
capitalization

Vocabulary
conflict resolution words

Grammar
articles
if statements

Technology
using a computer to create
   a slide show presentation

1. *Step 1: Buying vegetables*

2. _____

3. _____
_____
_____

4. _____
_____
_____

 Analyze Photos. Look at the photographs on this page and on page 121. Complete the following activities with a partner. The first one has been done for you.

1. Put the steps in this process in order by writing "Step 1", etc.

2. Label each step by describing what is happening in the picture.

3. What process do these pictures illustrate?

A **Read.** Read the process description.

How to Resolve a Conflict

What is a Conflict?

Before resolving a conflict, you need to decide if you have a conflict. A conflict is a disagreement between two or more people. Usually, the disagreement makes one of the disputants, or people, feel that his or her needs or interests are threatened. Often there is a misunderstanding in one or more parts of the disagreement. For example, Marta said that Tran could borrow her calculator over the weekend to finish some math homework. Tran lost Marta's calculator, and when he didn't give it back to her, Marta asked Tran where it was. Tran laughed and said he didn't know. Marta thought Tran was being very rude and inconsiderate for losing her calculator then laughing about it. She yelled at Tran and told him she would never loan him anything again. Tran yelled at Marta and told her she was being silly. "It's just a calculator!" he shouted. Marta walked away. Do Marta and Tran have a conflict? Yes. Now let's look at the steps involved in solving a conflict like Marta and Tran's.

Step 1: Communicate.

The first step to resolving almost all conflicts is for both parties, or people, to talk. Often just telling your side and hearing the other can resolve the conflict, because many conflicts are based on misunderstandings. However, sometimes one or both of the disputants need help talking and listening. If this is the case, the disputants look for a mediator. This is a person who helps the disputants each talk about their version of the conflict. In the case of Marta and Tran, they needed a mediator because both became angry when they tried to talk to each other. They agreed to meet with Ms. Nuñez, their English teacher. Ms. Nuñez helped Marta and Tran set the rules for their discussion. Each would have a chance to tell his or her version of the conflict while the other listened. Later, they would each have time to ask questions about the other person's version. Marta explained her version and said, "When I asked about it, he laughed." Ms. Nuñez asked how this made Marta feel. Marta said she felt like Tran didn't think her calculator was important. Then, Tran told his version. "When Marta asked me about it, I was nervous and laughed. I laugh when I'm nervous. Then, she yelled at me, so I got angry." Marta and Tran didn't have any questions for each other because they were beginning to understand the other person's point of view. However, they still hadn't solved their conflict.

Step 2: Find a Solution.

Next, the disputants find a solution to the conflict. If a rule is broken, then the solution can be to legislate, or set a new rule. Or the solution may be for one of the disputants to apologize if he or she has wronged the other disputant. Which solution would work better for Marta and Tran? Ms. Nuñez asked them to think about how to solve the conflict. Marta said she thought Tran should apologize and find or buy her a calculator. Tran agreed and said that Marta should apologize for yelling. Both of them apologized. Tran found Marta's calculator and returned it.

Step 3: Follow up.

After a solution has been reached, disputants should agree to follow up, or meet again, to check that the conflict has been resolved satisfactorily. Finally, Marta and Tran agreed to meet with Ms. Nuñez the next week. When they did, Marta had her calculator. She and Tran were good friends again. Conflict resolution can be difficult, but it is important. Finding solutions to problems helps people have strong, working relationships.

VOCABULARY

A Find each word in the reading on page 122. Look at the words around it to guess the meaning. Compare your answers with a partner.

Adjectives	Adverb	Nouns		Verbs
inconsiderate	satisfactorily	conflict	misunderstanding	borrow
rude		disagreement	party	legislate
threatened		disputant	side	resolve
		interest	version	
		mediator		

B Complete the sentences using the words from the box below.

side	~~disagreement~~	disputants	misunderstanding	satisfactorily
parties	version	mediator	resolve	

1. A conflict is a *disagreement* between two people.
2. The people who are in a conflict are often called the _____ or the _____ .
3. A _____ helps the people _____ the conflict.
4. Because conflicts are often the result of a _____ , listening is part of the solution.
5. The people involved tell their _____ or _____ of the story.
6. Then, they find a resolution that works _____ for both of them.

C Match the word with its definitions. Write the definitions next to the words.

1. conflict *e. problem; disagreement*   a. rights; things that are important to you
2. interests _____   b. not thinking of others
3. borrow _____   c. impolite; offensive
4. legislate _____   d. use something that belongs to another person
5. threatened _____   e. ~~problem; disagreement~~
6. rude _____   f. in danger or trouble
7. inconsiderate _____   g. people in a fight or conflict
8. disputants _____   h. make a rule or law

Articles	
Article	**Example Sentence**
a	A conflict is **a** disagreement between two or more people.
the	Usually, **the** disagreement makes one of **the** disputants, or people, feel that his or her needs or interests are threatened.
an	Tran and Marta made **an** agreement.

- The article *the* identifies something or someone definite.
- If you can answer the question *which one?* use *the*.
- Use *a* or *an* to talk about a nonspecific thing. Use *an* before nouns that start with a vowel sound. Use *a* before other nouns.

A Complete the sentences with the articles *a, an,* or *the*.

1. Before resolving _____*a*_____ conflict, you need to decide if you have _____*a*_____ conflict.

2. Often there is _____ misunderstanding in one or more parts of the disagreement.

3. _____ first step to resolving almost all conflicts is for both people, or parties, to talk.

4. Often just telling your side and hearing _____ other can resolve the conflict.

5. In _____ case of Marta and Tran, they needed a mediator because both became angry when they tried to talk to each other.

6. Ms. Nuñez helped Marta and Tran set _____ rules for their discussion.

7. Each party should have a chance to tell his or her version of _____ conflict.

8. This process should create _____ understanding between two disputants.

If Statements	
If at the beginning	**If at the end**
If a rule is broken, then the solution to legislate, or set a new rule.	The solution may be for one of the disputants to can be apologize **if** he or she has wronged the other disputant.

Use *if* clauses to talk about a possible situation and show what you think will happen. When the *if* clause comes at the beginning of a sentence, you must put a comma after the *if* clause. When the *if* clause comes at the end of the sentence, you do not use a comma.

B **Complete the sentences with your own words. Add commas if necessary.**

1. If someone calls you a name *, you should ignore it.* _____.

2. You should find a mediator if _____.

3. If someone borrows something of yours and loses it _____.

4. You should apologize if _____.

5. You should legislate if _____.

ORGANIZATION

Process Description/Sequential Essay

Complete the outline below with information from the reading on page 122.

> **Remember!**
> An **essay** has an introduction paragraph, body paragraphs, and a conclusion paragraph. In **sequential essays**, the introduction paragraph tells any steps you need to complete before beginning the process. It also defines any important terms and gives the example scenario. A sequential essay has as many body paragraphs as there are steps in the process. For example, if you are describing a three-step process, you will have three body paragraphs. The conclusion paragraph often tells the last step or what to do when the process is completed.

Conflict Resolution

I. **Introduction**

    A. Step(s) to complete before beginning the process: **1.** *Before resolving a conflict, you need to decide if you have a conflict.*

    B. Definition of terms: **2.** _____

    C. Introduction of the example scenario: **3.** _____

II. **Body Paragraph I**

    A. First step: **4.** _____

        1. Scenario example: **5.** _____

III. **Body Paragraph II**

    A. Second step: **6.** _____

        1. Scenario example: **7.** _____

IV. **Conclusion**

    A. Last step: **8.** _____

        1. Scenario example: **9.** _____

WRITING STRATEGIES

Sequence Words

Find the sequence words below in the reading on page 122. On the lines next to each sequence word, write the sentence from the reading that uses the word. Remember to include the commas.

Remember!
Use **sequence words** to show the order of steps in a process. Some common sequence words are *first, before, later, second, third, (etc.), then, since, finally, now, next, following,* and *after.* Use a comma after the sequence word or the phrase that includes it.

1. before _Before resolving a conflict, you need to decide if you have a conflict._ _____

   _____

2. first _____

   _____

3. then _____

   _____

4. later _____

   _____

5. now _____

   _____

6. finally _____

   _____

Using a Scenario for Support

Answer the following questions in complete sentences, using information from the reading on page 122.

Remember!
When you write about the steps in a process, it is helpful to use a **scenario**, or a specific example, to explain the process. After you describe each step, you can write how that step would be completed in the scenario.

1. Who are the disputants in the scenario?

   The disputants are Marta and Tran. _____

2. What is their conflict?

   _____

3. Who is their mediator?

   _____

4. What is their first step in resolving their conflict?

_____

_____

5. What is their second step?

_____

_____

6. What is their last step?

_____

_____

WRITING CONVENTIONS

Capitalization

The sentences below are not correct. Capital letters are missing. Rewrite the sentences changing lowercase letters to capital letters where necessary.

> **Remember!**
> Use capital letters:
> * at the beginning of sentences
> * names of specific people (Keiko)
> * names of specific places (Vermont)
> * names of specific things (The Washington Monument)
> * languages (Korean)
> * nationalities (Japanese)
> * titles of people (Mr.)
> * titles of texts (*Conflict Resolution*)
> * months of the year (January)
> * days of the week (Tuesday)

1. they agreed to meet with ms. nuñez, their english teacher, on friday.
   They agreed to meet with Ms. Nunez, their English teacher, on Friday.

2. ms. nuñez helped marta and tran set the rules for their discussion.

_____

3. marta and tran agreed to meet ms. nuñez the next week.

_____

4. when they did, marta had her calculator; she and tran were good friends again.

_____

5. now, marta and tran are starting a conflict resolution club at washington heights school.

_____

Process Description Essay

A process description essay is a nonfiction text, usually five or more paragraphs long. This kind of essay explains how to do something. The introduction paragraph introduces the process, tells any steps to be done before the process begins, defines any important terms, and introduces the scenario. Each body paragraph explains a step in the process. The conclusion either explains the last step or tells what needs to be done after the last step. Process description essays are often in brochures, manuals, or pamphlets.

  A **Read.** Read Choon-Yei's process description essay about creating a computer slide show presentation.

How to Create a Computer Slide Show
by Choon-Yei Wei

A computer slide show is a presentation of visual information such as pictures, graphs, diagrams, and words. The presentation is made and displayed on a computer. Many computer programs can help you create a computer slide show. You will learn the basics of how to create one in this manual.

Gather Information. The first step when creating a computer slide show is gathering the information you want to include in your presentation. Let's say you are creating a presentation for a science fair. You will need to gather all the charts, graphs, and diagrams you used or created for the project. You also need all the results or facts you discovered during your project. Then, think about what you want to tell people about your project. That information can be typed into slides.

Create Your Slides. Most computer slide show programs include suggestions for how to design the best slide show for your needs. Some programs even present questions for you to answer so the program can make accurate suggestions for your particular presentation. Other programs provide templates, which are designs that are already created by the program. For your first computer slide show, you may want to use your program's suggestions or templates to make the process easier. If you are choosing a design that is right for a science fair presentation, you might choose a formal design with interesting but not distracting colors. Then, determine the layout, or order of the slides: Will you have a title slide first, followed by a picture of your experiment? Will you include a chart or a diagram next?

Remember Some Important Things. As you make your slides, remember several important things: 1. This is a visual presentation, so your slides should be visually interesting. 2. Keep all writing short and clear. 3. Be sure all graphs, charts, and diagrams are clearly labeled. 4. As you design each slide, be sure you like the color of the background and the size and color of the type. Most programs come with a very helpful manual to help you accomplish these tasks and use each feature. 5. Remember to save your slide show frequently! You don't want to lose your hard work.

Revise and Edit. When you have completed all the slides, go back and ask yourself if each one is visually interesting. Is the information clearly and accurately presented? Does the order of the slides make sense? Next, reread each slide to make sure there are no typos or errors. Ask another person to check your slides for mistakes. Finally, decide if you are going to present the slide show or let it run by itself. If you present it, use tools such as arrows to click through each slide. Practice using the tools and explaining each slide. If you want the slide show to run by itself, as for a science fair, find that option in the tools. Set the amount of time that each slide displays. Watch the slide show several times to make sure everything runs smoothly. Be sure you show your slide show to at least one other person before presenting it to a group. Using a computer slide show can greatly enhance any presentation. Now you are ready to begin!

B **Summarize.** Re-read Choon-Yei's essay on computer slide shows. Label each picture below with a brief summary of the step it shows. The first has been done for you.

I.

The first step is to gather the information you

want to present.

III.

_____

_____

_____

II.

_____

_____

_____

_____

IV.

_____

_____

_____

_____

STEP-BY-STEP WRITING

Purpose: Describe a Process

WRITING PROMPT

Write a sequential essay that describes a process. Share the essay with your teacher and classmates.

✔ Prompt Checklist

❏ I read the task carefully.
❏ I understood the form, audience, topic, and purpose of the prompt.

STEP 1 Pre-write

A Look at Choon-Yei's list of possible topics. Make your own list.

Choon-Yei's List

How to make bool kolgi
How to do origami
How to make charts on the computer
How to make graphs on the computer
How to make computer slide shows
How to build a birdhouse

B After you have chosen the process you want to describe, complete the process yourself. If this is not possible, pantomime, draw, or read about the process. Then, record each step of the process in order.

Step 1: Gather information.

Step 2: Create your slides.

Step 3: Remember some important things: make slides visually interesting; use short and clear writing; label all graphs, charts, and diagrams; and choose backgrounds.

Step 4: Revise and edit.

Step 5: Give your presentation.

STEP 2 Organize

Look at Choon-Yei's outline. Make your own outline about the process you chose.

Choon-Yei's Outline

Title: How to Create a Computer Slide Show

I. Introduction

    A. Definition of terms: A computer slide show is a presentation of visual information such as pictures, graphs, diagrams, and words. The presentation is made and displayed on a computer.

II. Body Paragraph I

    A. Step 1: Gather information

        1. Scenario example: Science fair: Gather all the charts, graphs, and diagrams you used or made and the facts you discovered.

III. Body Paragraph II

    A. Step 2: Create your slides (Use the computer program's suggestions or templates.)

        1. Scenario example: Choose a design that is right for a science fair—formal. Then, decide the layout.

IV. Body Paragraph III

    A. Step 3: Remember some important things

        1. Scenario example: Make slides interesting, short, and clear. Choose appropriate type, size, and color.

V. Conclusion

    A. Step 4: Revise and edit

        1. Scenario example: Reread, present to another person, and edit each slide.

STEP 3 Draft and Revise

A **Practice.** Look at Choon-Yei's first draft. How can she improve it? Answer the questions.

First Draft
How to Create a Computer Slide Show
by Choon-Yei Wei

(1) The computer slide show is a presentation of visual information such as pictures, graphs, diagrams, and words. (2) The presentation is made and displayed on a computer. (3) Many computer programs can help you create a computer slide show. (4) You will learn the basics of how to create one in this manual.

gather information.

(5) The first step when creating a computer slide show is gathering the information you want to include in your presentation. (6) Let's say you are creating a presentation for a science fair. (7) You will need to gather all the charts, graphs, and diagrams you used or created for the project. (8) You also need all the results or facts you discovered during your project. (9) Then, think about what you want to tell people about your project. (10) That information can be typed into slides.

Create Your Slides.

(11) Most computer slide show programs include suggestions for how to design the best slide show for your needs. (12) Some programs even present questions for you to answer so the program can make accurate suggestions for your particular presentation. (13) Other programs provide templates, which are designs that are already created by the program. (14) For your first computer slide show, you may want to use your program's suggestions or templates to make the process easier. (15) In planning a science fair presentation, you might choose a formal design with interesting but not distracting colors. (16) Determine the layout, or order of the slides: Will you have a title slide first, followed by a picture of your experiment? (17) Will you include a chart or a diagram next?

Remember Some Important Things.

(18) As you make your slides, remember several important things: 1. This is a visual presentation, so your slides should be visually interesting. 2. Keep all writing short and clear. 3. Be sure all graphs, charts, and diagrams are clearly labeled. 4. As you design each slide, be sure you like the color of the background and the size and color of the type. (19) Most programs come with a very helpful manual to help you accomplish these tasks and use each feature. (20) Remember to save your slide show frequently! (21) You don't want to lose your hard work.

Revise and Finalize.

(22) When you have completed all the slides, go back and ask yourself if each one is visually interesting. (23) Is the

information clearly and accurately presented? (24) Does the order
of the slides make sense? (25) Next, reread each slide to make
sure there are no typos or errors. (26) Ask another person to
check your slides for mistakes. (27) Decide if you are going to
present the slide show or let it run by itself. (28) If you
present it, use tools such as arrows, to click through each
slide. (29) Practice using the tools and explaining each slide.
(30) If you want the slide show to run by itself find that option
in the tools. (31) Set the amount of time that each slide
displays. (32) Watch the slide show several times to make sure
everything runs smoothly. (33) Be sure you show your slide show
to at least one other person before presenting it to a group.
(34) Using a computer slide show can greatly enhance any
presentation. (35) Now you are ready to begin!

1. How can Choon-Yei best improve sentence 1?
   A Change *The* to *A*.
   B Change *The* to *An*.
   C Change *The* to *a*.
   D Change *The* to *the*.

2. How can Choon-Yei best improve the first subtitle?
   A Change *gather information* to *Gather information*.
   B Change *gather information* to *Gather Information*.
   C Change *gather information* to *gather Information*.
   D Change *gather information* to *GATHER INFORMATION*.

3. How can Choon-Yei best rewrite sentence 15 to include an *if* clause?
   A If for a science fair presentation, you might choose a formal design with interesting but not distracting colors.
   B If you are choosing a design that is right for a science fair presentation you might choose a formal design with interesting but not distracting colors.
   C If you are choosing a design that is right for a science fair presentation, you might choose a formal design with interesting but not distracting colors.

   D You might choose a formal design with interesting but not distracting colors, if you are choosing a design that is right for a science fair presentation.

4. What word can Choon-Yei add to the beginning of sentence 16 to show sequential order?
   A First,
   B Before,
   C Since,
   D Then,

5. What word can Choon-Yei add to the beginning of sentence 27 to show sequential order?
   A Second,
   B Finally,
   C Following,
   D After,

6. What phrase should Choon-Yei add after the word *itself* in sentence 30 to include a reference to the scenario?
   A as for a science fair,
   B , or automatically,
   C , a computer,
   D , like slide shows,

B **Draft.** Write a first draft of your process description essay. Use your notes from Steps 1 and 2.

C **Revise.** Read your first draft. How can you improve it? Look at the revision checklist. Revise your writing.

STEP 4 Edit

A **Practice.** Read the sentences. Choose the best substitute for the underlined words. If the sentence is correct, choose "Make no change."

1. Origami is the <u>ancient</u> art of folding paper to make shapes.
   A Ancient art
   B Ancient Art
   C ancient Art
   (D) Make no change.

2. If you want to make a bird in <u>origami follow</u> these simple directions.
   A origami, follow
   B origami. follow
   C origami; follow
   D Make no change.

3. <u>After</u>, make or find a square piece of paper with one side white and one side colored.
   A Before,
   B Next,
   C First,
   D Make no change.

4. <u>Then</u>, fold one corner up to form a white triangle.
   A Later,
   B Since,
   C Third,
   D Make no change.

5. You should use your <u>thumbnail, if</u> you want a sharp crease.
   A thumbnail if
   B thumbnail; if
   C thumbnail. if
   D Make no change.

6. Next, unfold <u>a</u> paper and fold up the other corner to make another white triangle.
   A an
   B the
   C and
   D Make no change.

7. Turn the paper over. You should see a big x like the intersection of Main Street and <u>oak street</u>.
   A Oak street
   B oak Street
   C Oak Street
   D Make no change.

8. Now, fold the paper from left to right to make <u>the</u> rectangle.
   A a
   B an
   C and
   D Make no change.

B **Edit.** Re-read your draft from Step 3. Look at the editing checklist. Edit your writing.

 C **Peer Edit.** Exchange drafts with a partner. Tell your partner what you like about the draft. Look at the editing checklist. Tell your partner how to improve the draft.

✓ Editing Checklist

me	my partner	
❏	❏	used capital letters correctly
❏	❏	used sequence words correctly
❏	❏	used articles correctly
❏	❏	used *if* clauses correctly

STEP 5 Publish

Rewrite your process description essay in your best handwriting or use a computer. Look at Choon-Yei's essay on page 128 for ideas. Present your process description essay to the class.

TECHNOLOGY

Using a Computer to Create a Slide Show Presentation

 Reread Choon-Yei's essay on page 128. Follow her advice step by step.

- Create a slide show presentation of your process description.
  - Slide 1 should be the title of your essay and your name.
  - Slide 2 should summarize the introduction paragraph.
  - Slide 3 should summarize your first body paragraph, etc.
- You may need to use more than one slide for each paragraph.
- Also, try to create and insert appropriate visuals such as pictures, diagrams, or charts.
- Present your slide show to the class.

GROUP WRITING

Work in a group to write about one of these topics. Follow the steps below.

1. Choose your topic.
2. Discuss and record information.
3. Do research, if you need to.
4. Write a first draft.
5. Revise and edit the draft with your group.
6. Present your group's essay to the class.

Topic 1

Write a response to literature essay about a short story or novel you have read. Briefly tell the plot of the story. Then describe the strengths and weaknesses of the story, giving examples from the text to support each point.

Topic 2

Write a process description essay. Explain to your reader how to do something in steps. Give examples for each step.

TIMED WRITING

Choose one writing prompt. Complete the writing task in 45 minutes.

WRITING PROMPT 1

Write a five-paragraph response to literature essay about a short story or novel you have read. Briefly tell the plot of the story. Then describe the strengths and weaknesses of the story, giving examples from the text to support each point.

WRITING PROMPT 2

Write a process description essay about something you know how to do. Explain to your reader how to do something in steps. Give examples for each step.

 Test Tip

Examples! Remember to include specific examples to support each point or step in your essay. The examples can be quotes from a story or a person, stories of personal experience, or facts.

SELF-CHECK

Think about your writing skills. Check (✔) the answers that are true.

1. I understand. . .
   - ❑ literary analysis words.
   - ❑ conflict resolution words.

2. I can correctly. . .
   - ❑ combine information with relative clauses.
   - ❑ connect ideas with transition words.
   - ❑ use sequence words.
   - ❑ use a scenario for support.

3. I can correctly. . .
   - ❑ use past perfect tense.
   - ❑ use articles.
   - ❑ use *if*-statements.

4. I can correctly. . .
   - ❑ summarize.
   - ❑ capitalize.

5. I can organize my writing. . .
   - ❑ with a three-part thesis statement.
   - ❑ in sequential order.
   - ❑ step by step.

6. I can write to. . .
   - ❑ analyze literature.
   - ❑ describe a process.

Unit 9

Argue a Point

1. *Volunteering in a hospital*

PRE-READING

Analyze Photos. Look at the photographs on this page and on page 138. Label each picture. Describe what is happening. The first one has been done for you.

2. _____

3. _____

4. _____

A **Read.** Read the persuasive essay.

Volunteer—One Change Makes a Big Difference

You don't have to look far to see the problems in this world. The evening news, adults whispering and clicking their tongues, and newspaper headlines tell about war, broken communities, the polluted environment, and suffering people around the world and in our own backyard. You may want to close your eyes and ignore all the problems. After all, you are just one person and there are so many problems. But that would be the same as not taking care of an illness. However, I believe that if each of us volunteers and makes only one change, the world will become a better place.

Volunteering means to work for someone or something without getting paid. You may not earn any money while volunteering, but in my opinion, you will gain much more than you give. Perhaps you do not think you have the talent to volunteer, but there is surely something worthwhile you can do for others. When you volunteer, you will find hidden talents and abilities you never knew you had. You will also discover the intrinsic, or natural, rewards in making a change in the world.

Studies have shown that volunteering is good for you! The Corporation for National and Community Service reports that "those who volunteer have lower mortality rates, greater functional ability, and lower rates of depression later in life than those who do not volunteer" (Health Benefits). Other studies have shown that teens who volunteer have higher self-esteem. A study from Cincinnati Children's Hospital shows that "teens who do volunteer activities, for example, often feel better about themselves and have a higher self-esteem because they have made a difference in someone else's life" (Teen Stressors). It seems to me that if you volunteer, you will have a healthier body and mind and the world will become a healthier place, too.

You may argue that you don't have the time, talent, or interests to volunteer. I have found that there are so many volunteer opportunities that one or more will certainly fit your schedule, abilities, and interest. One Web site directory lists forty different volunteer opportunities. Some are even available from the comfort of your home. However, it is my opinion that the best volunteer opportunities allow you to meet other people, especially those you are serving. If you are interested in animals, for example, you should volunteer in animal shelters, zoos, or veterinary hospitals where you will meet people who also like animals. Last year, I volunteered at an animal shelter and had a very rewarding experience. I even adopted a dog! If you are interested in the environment, you can volunteer with one of many organizations dedicated to sustaining and protecting a healthy environment. Are you interested in helping young children? Your local library or school would be happy to have you volunteer some time and energy with young children. Maybe you think helping the poor or needy is crucial. If so, you can work in a food pantry, a prison, or a homeless shelter. I feel that the opportunities are endless.

Some volunteer organization or project needs your help, and you can make a difference. When you think about where to volunteer, first think about your interests. Is there a cause or problem in the world that you pay attention to or care a lot about? What issues compel you? Next, do some Internet or library research to find a good fit for you. Then, don't wait! Begin volunteering today. According to the Corporation for National and Community Service, fifty-five percent of all teens volunteer. That is nearly double the rate of adults who volunteer (Kujawski). Teens are leading the way to changing the world, one volunteer at a time. Won't you join them?

Sources:
Kujawski, Laura. "First Lady Releases Study Showing High Levels of Teen Volunteerism." <u>PNN Online</u>. 1 Dec. 2005. 3 Aug. 2007 <http://pnnonline.org/article.php?sid=6374>.
"The Health Benefits of Volunteering: A Review of Recent Research." Corporation for National and Community Service, Office of Research and Policy Development. Apr. 2007. 5 Aug. 2007 <http://www.nationalservice.gov/about/role_impact/performance_research.asp#HBR>.
"Teen Stressors." Cincinnati Children's Hospital Medical Center. 5 Aug. 2007 <http://www.cincinnatichildrens.org/svc/alpha/p/psychiatry/teens/real-life/self-esteen.htm>.

VOCABULARY

A Find each word in the reading on page 140. Look at the words around it to guess the meaning. Compare your answers with a partner's.

Adjectives	Nouns	Verbs
crucial	depression	compel
endless	self-esteem	gain
intrinsic	talent	ignore
overwhelming		sustain
polluted		whisper
suffering		volunteer
whispering		
worthwhile		
volunteer		

B Match the word with its definition. Write the definitions next to the words.

1. sustain _____ a. ~~convince; have powerful effect~~

2. gain _____ b. to work without pay

3. intrinsic _____ c. ability

4. crucial _____ d. natural

5. compel *a. convince; have powerful effect* e. support to keep in existence

6. self-esteem _____ f. get; earn

7. talent _____ g. how you feel about yourself

8. volunteer _____ h. very important

C Complete the sentences using the words from the box below. Use the appropriate form of the word.

depression	endless	ignore	pollute	suffer	~~whispering~~

1. When you don't want others to hear, you _____*whisper*_____ quietly.

2. Animals that are _____ need our help.

3. Factories and cars have _____ our environment.

4. People who are sad all the time suffer from _____.

5. When you _____ a problem, it doesn't go away.

6. The ways to help are _____.

Modals	
Modal Verb	**Purpose**
You **may** want to close your eyes.	to express possibility
You **will** gain much more than you give.	to show future certainty
There is surely something worthwhile you **can** do for others.	to show ability
You **should** volunteer in animal shelters, zoos, or hospitals.	to make a recommendation or suggestion

Modals are also called helping or auxiliary verbs. They help form the tense and voice of the main verb. Modals are special verbs because:

- They have different purposes. See the chart above.
- They do not take *s* in the third person. *She **may** want to close her eyes.*
- They do not change form to show tense. *You should have volunteered with us yesterday.*
- You use "not" to make modals negative. *You **may not** want to close your eyes.*

A Re-read the essay on page 140. Find examples of the following modals. Write an example sentence. The first has been done for you.

1. can *It can be overwhelming.* _____

2. may not _____

_____

3. may _____

_____

4. should _____

_____

5. can _____

_____

Future Conditionals

If / When at the beginning	If / When at the end
If each of us volunteers and makes only one change, the world **will** become a better place.	The world **will** become a better place **if** we volunteer.
When you volunteer, you **will** find hidden talents and abilities you never knew you had.	You **will** find hidden talents and abilities you never knew you had **when** you volunteer.

The future conditional is used to show possibility in the future.

To form the future conditional, use:

If/When + simple present tense verb . . . *will* + verb.
If we volunteer and make *only one change, the world* **will become** *a better place.*

OR

will + verb . . . . *if / when* + simple present tense verb
You will find *hidden talents and abilities you never knew you had* **when you volunteer**.
Remember that when the *if / when* clause comes at the beginning of a sentence, you must put a comma after the *if / when* clause. When the *if / when* clause comes at the end of the sentence, you do not use a comma.

B Complete the sentences with your own words. Add commas where necessary.

1. If we volunteer, *we will help people and might learn a lot.* _____

2. When you volunteer _____
   _____.

3. _____
   _____ you will have a healthier body and mind.

4. If you work at an animal hospital _____
   _____.

5. _____
   _____ when you work with young children.

Persuasive Essay

Complete the outline below with information from the reading on page 140.

Volunteer—One Change Makes a Big Difference

I. **Introduction Paragraph 1**

    A. Getting the reader's attention:

        1. *You don't have to look far to see the problems in this world.* _____

        _____

    B. Explains writer's opinion:

        2. _____

        _____

II. **Introduction Paragraph 2**

    C. Define terms: 3. _____

    _____

III. **Body Paragraph I**

    A. Explain a positive point: 4. _____

        1. Evidence: 5. _____

        _____

        2. Evidence: 6. _____

        _____

IV. **Body Paragraph II**

    A. Argue against a point: 7. _____

        1. Evidence: 8. _____

        _____

V. **Conclusion**

    A. Summary: 9. _____

    _____

    B. Challenge to reader: 10. _____

    _____

WRITING STRATEGIES

Sorting Out Reasons

Re-read the essay on page 140. List the argument and the three main points that the writer makes. The first one has been done for you. Place an asterisk next to any points that are counterpoints, or arguments against a reader's beliefs.

Re-read the essay on page 140.

Remember!
In a persuasive essay, you give reasons for your opinions. Most arguments have two sides—for and against—so it's important for you to **sort out your reasons** before you present them in your essay. You can do this by listing positive and negative reasons to answer a question about your topic.

1. argument: *If each of us volunteers and makes only one change, the world will become a better place.*

2. first point: _____
   _____

3. second point: _____
   _____

4. third point: _____
   _____

Using Analogies, Anecdotes, and Evidence to Support an Argument

Find different kinds of support in the reading on page 140. Record the sentence that gives the support. Tell what kind of support it is by labeling it *analogy, anecdote,* or *evidence.* The first has been done for you.

Find different kinds of support in the reading on page 140.

Remember!
There are many ways to support your opinions in a persuasive essay.

- You can use **analogies**, or comparisons between two situations: *Volunteering is like caring for your family, except the whole world becomes your family.*
- You can use **anecdotes**, or personal stories: *When I volunteered at a soup kitchen, I learned to appreciate the food my mother and father cook for me.*
- You can use **evidence**, or facts: *Fifty-five percent of all teens volunteer.*

1. *"Those who volunteer have lower mortality rates, greater functional ability, and lower rates of depression later in life than those who do not volunteer."(evidence)*

2. _____
   _____

3. _____
   _____

4. _____
   _____

WRITING CONVENTIONS

Using Words that Signal Opinion

Find the opinion signal words in the reading on page 140. Record the sentence that contains the word and circle the signal words. The first one has been done for you.

1. *However, (I believe) that if each of us volunteers and makes only one change, the world will become a better place.*

2. _____.

3. _____.

4. _____.

5. _____.

6. _____.

WRITING

Persuasive Essay

A **persuasive essay** is a nonfiction text, usually five or more paragraphs long. This kind of essay tries to convince the reader of something.

The introduction paragraph introduces the topic or question that the writer will argue, gives any background information needed, and gives the writer's position or opinion on the topic.

Each body paragraph explains a point in the argument and supports it with reasons in the form of analogies, anecdotes, or evidence.

The conclusion summarizes the writer's position and the three main points presented in the body paragraphs. The conclusion usually includes a final suggestion for the reader.

Persuasive essays usually appear in newspaper editorial pages or letters to the editor.

The Benefits of Year-Round Schooling

by Alma Suarez

Are you stressed by the quick pace of our school year? Do you get tired or burnt out going to school from fall to spring with only one week off each season? Do you feel like your brain goes to sleep during the summer and it takes a long time for it to wake up? Are you worried that students from other countries are getting far ahead of American students? If you answered yes to any of these questions, then I have the solution for you: year-round schooling. Don't let the name scare you. Year-round schooling does not mean going to school all year long without a break. It means going to school for a few months, then taking a short one- or two-week break, then going to school for a few more months, then taking another break…all year round. The traditional school schedule was invented when Americans were mainly farmers. Students had to have summers off to help on their family's farms. Now, most Americans are not farmers, and students do not need summers off. I believe that year-round schooling provides more time for learning, helps teachers and students feel well rested, and improves test scores.

Schools that use the year-round schedule have found that teachers and students are able to spend time more time on learning. It seems to me that they don't feel rushed by the short school year. One teacher, Carla Kolodey, described her feelings about the year-round schedule in a California district. "You get less burned out. Right when you start feeling overwhelmed, you get a break" (Kenning). Tom Carter, a principal in a nearby school, described the same effect on students. He claims the breaks are crucial for his students. The traditional schedule was discouraging. "For our kids, to sit for an 18-week semester, they really struggled," Carter said. "They'd get frustrated and cut class" (Kenning).

People on the year-round schedule feel well rested after their breaks and ready to learn again for a few months. However, in my opinion, they don't take such long breaks that they forget everything they learned. Dr. Harris Cooper, a professor at Duke University, studied "summer regression." He looked at standardized test scores taken before and after summer. He found that "children on average lost about a month of grade level achievement score" (Messina). Over the years, students lose a whole year or more of learning. No wonder other countries are ahead of us on tests and achievement!

These year-round educators are also finding that their test scores are improving. Although only four percent of this nation's schools have implemented year-round schooling, studies show that these schools have improved academically. The year-round Oxnard school district of California has conducted a nine-year study that shows improved test scores (MacNeil-Lehrer).

Therefore, if you feel stressed or over tired during the school year or are concerned about keeping up with students in other countries, year-round schooling will help. If you are worried you will miss summer camp or summer job opportunities, you should consider that most year-round schedules include a four- to six-week summer break to allow for these opportunities. Why not start now? The benefits are compelling.

Sources:

"Going to School Year-Round." MacNeil-Lehrer Productions. 8 Aug. 2001. 5 Aug. 2007 <http://www.pbs.org/newshour/extra/features/july-dec01/year-round.html>.

Kenning, Chris. "Teachers See Benefits in Year-Round Schools." The Courier Journal. 17 July 2006. 5 Aug. 2007 <http://www.nayre.org/Louisville%20CJ%20July%2017.pdf>.

Messina, Ignazio. "Summer Regression." The Toledo Blade. 7 Aug. 2006. 5 Aug. 2007 <http://www.nayre.org/Toledo%20Blade%208%2007.pdf>.

B Reread Alma's essay on year-round schooling on page 147. Label each picture below with a brief summary of the supporting point it shows. The first one has been done for you.

I.

Teachers and students at year-round schools are less stressed and happier.

II.

III.

_____

_____

_____

_____

STEP-BY-STEP WRITING

Purpose: Argue a Point

WRITING PROMPT

Write a persuasive essay on an opinion you feel strongly about. Share the essay with your teacher and classmates.

✔ **Prompt Checklist**

☐ I read the task carefully.
☐ I understood the form, audience, topic, and purpose of the prompt.

STEP 1 Pre-write

A Look at Alma's list of possible topics. Make your own list.

Alma's List of Topics

school uniforms in public schools	ending cigarette sales anywhere in the US
female professional sports teams	age limits on CDs and video games
(year-round schooling)	busing to integrate schools

After you have chosen the point you want to argue, consider what analogies, anecdotes, and evidence you will use to support your point. Also ask yourself what arguments your reader might make against your points. Look at Alma's web below. Make your own web.

Alma's Web

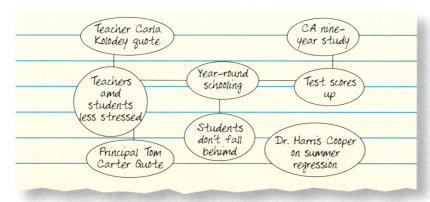

STEP 2 Organize

B Look at Alma's outline. Make your own outline for your persuasive essay.

Title: The Benefits of Year-Round Schooling

I. Introduction

   A. Attention grabber: *Are you stressed by the quick pace of our school year?*

   B. Definition of terms: *Year-round schooling does not mean going to school all year long without a break. It means going to school for a few months, then taking a short one- or two- week break, then going to school for a few more months, then taking another break…all year round.*

   C. Statement of opinion with three main points: *I believe that year-round schooling provides more time for learning, helps teachers and students feel well rested, and improves test scores.*

II. Body Paragraph I

   A. Topic sentence: *Schools that use the year-round schedule have found that teachers and students are able to spend time more time on learning.*

   1. Support: Teacher Carla Kolodey quote

   2. Support: Principal Tom Carter quote

III. Body Paragraph II

    A. Topic sentence: *People on the year-round schedule feel well rested after their breaks and ready to learn again for a few months.*

        1. Support: Dr. Harris Cooper quote

IV. Body Paragraph III

    A. Topic sentence: *These year-round educators are also finding that their test scores are improving.*

        1. Support: California 9-year study

V. Conclusion

    A. Summarize points: *Therefore, if you feel stressed or over-tired during the school year or are concerned about keeping up with students in other countries, year-round schooling will help.*

    B. Make suggestion: *Why not start now?*

STEP 3 Draft and Revise

 A **Practice.** **Look at Alma's first draft. How can she improve it? Answer the questions.**

First Draft

The Benefits of Year-Round Schooling

by Alma Suarez

(1) Year-round schooling does not mean going to school all year long without a break. (2) It means going to school for a few months, then taking a short one- or two- week break, then going to school for a few more months, then taking another break...all year round. (3) The traditional school schedule was invented when Americans were mainly farmers. (4) Students had to have summers off to help on their family's farms. (5) Now, most Americans are not farmers, and students do not need summers off. (6) I believe that year-round schooling provides more time for learning, helps teachers and students feel well rested, and improves test scores.

(7) Schools that use the year-round schedule have found that teachers and students are able to spend time more time on learning. (8) They don't feel rushed by the short school year. (9) One teacher, Carla Kolodey, described her feelings about the year-round schedule in a California district: (10) "You get less burned out. (11) Right when you start feeling overwhelmed, you get a break" (Kenning). (12) Tom Carter, a principal in a nearby school, described the same effect on students. (13) He claims the breaks are crucial for his students. (14) The traditional schedule was discouraging. (15) "For our kids, to sit for an 18-week semester, they really struggled," Carter said. (16) "They'd get frustrated and cut class" (Kenning).

(17) People on the year-round schedule feel well rested after their breaks and ready to learn again for a few months. (18) However, in my opinion, they don't take such long breaks that they forget everything they learned. (19) Over the years, students lose a whole year or more of learning. (20) No wonder other countries are ahead of us on tests and achievement!

(21) These year-round educators are also finding that their test scores are improving. (22) Although only four percent of this nation's schools have implemented year-round schooling, studies show that these schools have improved academically. (23) The year-round Oxnard school district of California has conducted a nine-year study that shows improved test scores (MacNeil-Lehrer).

(24) Therefore, if you feel stressed or over-tired during the school year or are concerned about keeping up with students in other countries, year-round schooling is helping you. (25) If you are worried you will miss summer camp or summer job opportunities, consider that most year-round schedules include a four- to six-week summer break to allow for these opportunities.

1. How can Alma best improve paragraph 1?
   A Add support.
   B Add opinion signal words.
   C Add sentences that get the reader's attention.
   D Add a definition of year-round schooling.

2. How can Alma improve sentence 8?
   A Add *It seems to me that* to the beginning.
   B Add *It seems to me that* to the end.
   C Add *My belief* to the beginning.
   D Add *my belief* to the end.

3. How can Alma best improve paragraph 3?
   A Add support.
   B Add opinion signal words.
   C Add sentences that get the reader's attention.
   D Add a definition of year-round schooling.

4. How can Alma rewrite sentence 24 to show future conditional?
   A Change *you feel stressed* to *you are feeling stressed.*
   B Change *you feel stressed* to *you felt stressed.*
   C Change *is helping you* to *will help you.*
   D Change *is helping you* to *willing help you.*

5. How can Alma rewrite sentence 25 to use a modal?
   A Add *will* before *consider.*
   B Add *you should* before *consider.*
   C Add *you can* before *consider.*
   D Add *you will* before *consider.*

6. How can Alma improve paragraph 5?
   A Add support.
   B Add opinion signal words.
   C Add a summary of the points.
   D Add a suggestion or challenge to the reader.

B **Draft.** Write a first draft of your persuasive essay. Use your notes from Steps 1 and 2.

C **Revise.** Read your first draft. How can you improve it? Look at the revision checklist. Revise your writing.

☑ **Revision Checklist**

❑ I wrote an introduction, body paragraphs, and a conclusion paragraph.
❑ I got the reader's attention.
❑ I introduced the issue and my three points.
❑ I defined important terms.
❑ I included opinion words.
❑ I used analogies, anecdotes, or evidence to support my points.
❑ I used future conditional and modals correctly.

STEP 4 Edit

A **Practice.** Read the sentences. Choose the best word or phrase to complete each sentence.

1. Are you tired of unhealthy school lunches? Do you think schools _____ have to provide well-balanced meals?
   A can
   B should
   C will
   D may

2. I _____ that the food you eat at school should be nutritious.
   A believe
   B seem
   C found
   D want

3. If schools prepare healthy meals, students _____ better.
   A will study
   B wills studying
   C are studying
   D are study

4. If schools provide whole grain snacks, students _____ tired at the end of the day.
   A not will become
   B will not become
   C will become not
   D became

5. It _____ to me that schools can use less fat in their foods.
   A belief
   B idea
   C seems
   D understand

6. Studies have shown that healthy eating is _____ to brain development.
   A crucial
   B talent
   C suffering
   D overwhelming

7. Possibly, schools _____ find that they don't have to spend more money to provide healthy food.
   A can
   B will
   C should
   D may

8. Remember, a healthy body image is a big part of a student's _____.
   A volunteer
   B talent
   C self-esteem
   D depression

B **Edit.** Re-read your draft from Step 3. Look at the editing checklist. Is everything correct? Edit your writing.

 Peer Edit. Exchange drafts with a partner. Tell your partner what you like about the draft. Look at the editing checklist. Tell your partner how to improve

 Editing Checklist

	my	
me	partner	
❏	❏	used modals correctly
❏	❏	used opinion words correctly
❏	❏	used future conditionals correctly
❏	❏	used vocabulary correctly

the draft.

STEP 5 Publish

Rewrite your persuasive essay in your best handwriting or use a computer. Look at Alma's essay

on page 147 for ideas. Present your persuasive essay to the class.

Using a Computer to Find Personal Anecdotes

Personal anecdotes or stories are often good support for a supporting point in a persuasive essay. However, you may not have any personal experience with the topic you are arguing. So you may need to read about and summarize another person's personal anecdote. To find personal anecdotes, you can:

- Do a keyword search: Go to your favorite search engine. Type your topic into the search line. If too many Web sites come up, use quotes around the topic to refine your search. Read the first page of Web sites, looking for names of specific people or places.

Unit 10

Information Essay

UNIT OBJECTIVES

Writing
information essay

Organization
main idea and details

Writing Strategies
varying sentence structure

Writing Conventions
using colons

Vocabulary
space words

Grammar
adjective clauses

Technology
using a computer to research
   a topic

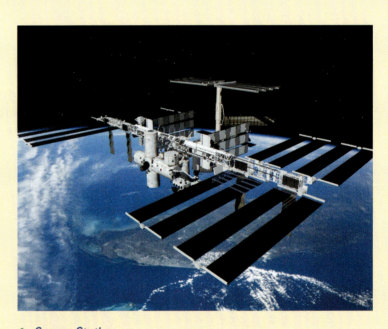

1. *Space Station*

PRE-READING

Analyze Photos. Look at the photographs on this page and on page 154. With a partner, describe the pictures. Try to name and describe everything you see by making educated guesses. Label each picture.

2. _____

3. _____

4. _____

A **Read.** Read the information essay.

The International Space Station

The International Space Station (ISS) is well named. It is truly international: more than fifteen countries are helping to build it. It is an enormous satellite orbiting, or circling, the Earth. Like a train station in space, people stay there for a short time—from a few days to six months (Gallant 19). However, unlike a train station, the space station is their destination. There, astronauts learn to live in space. They conduct science experiments. The ISS allows people to live and study in space in ways they never have before. To understand the importance of the ISS, one must know its history, design, and mission.

As with many new endeavors, the International Space Station's history is long and bumpy. The ISS is the ninth space station. The first six were built by the Soviet Union. They were called the Saylut Stations. They were built in the 1970s. During this time, the United States also built a space station. It was called Sky Lab. In 1986, the Soviet Union launched Mir. This space station was the largest and most successful of all. It lasted more than ten years. Many astronauts from around the world and cosmonauts from the Soviet Union went to Mir to study space. In the 1990s, Russia planned to build a Mir 2. Meanwhile, the United States with Canada, Europe, and Japan planned to build a space station, which they would call Freedom. However, neither group had enough money. In 1993, all of these countries decided to build a space station together (Oberg).

The International Space Station was designed to be assembled in parts. The parts are called modules. Each module is sent into space and connected to the other modules. In November of 1998, Russia sent the first module, Zarya, into space. Zarya means "sunrise" in Russian. A month later, the United States sent the module Unity to be connected to Zarya. Unity has six hatches. One connects to Zarya, and the others will connect to other modules. In July of 2000, Russia sent the Zvezda module. Zvezda means "star." This is where the cosmonauts and astronauts live and work. Three months later, the United States sent solar panels and other large equipment up to the space station. The solar panels give the station its electricity. Now the space station was ready to be inhabited. The first crew to live and work on the International Space Station was American astronaut Sam Shepherd and Russian cosmonauts Yuri Gidzenko and Sergei Krikalev.

These men began to fulfill the mission of the International Space Station: to "enable long-term exploration of space and provide benefits to people on Earth" (Greene). What this means is that the astronauts and cosmonauts who visit the space station conduct scientific experiments. Some of the experiments are related to space: how humans can live in space, how weightlessness affects biological specimens, etc. Other experiments are related to medicine: how protein crystals grow in space, for example. As researcher Roy A. Gallant states, "the knowledge that can be gained from space stations is endless" (Gallant 31).

Since its beginning, the International Space Station has been an endeavor that has brought people together throughout the world. Astronauts, cosmonauts, and scientists from many different countries have visited and worked on the space station. Engineers and designers from all over the world have helped to build the modules and other space station equipment. However, the future of the space station is insecure. In 2001, the United States ran out of money for the space station. NASA decided to stop building new modules for the space station. Then on February 1, 2003, the American space shuttle Columbia crashed. All seven crewmembers died. The United States stopped all space flights until it could be sure they would be safe. Will the space station be completed with all eight modules? Will large crews of astronauts, cosmonauts, and scientists study at the space station? If not, then the world will lose one of its most valuable resources: the International Space Station.

Sources:

Gallant, Roy A. Space Stations. New York: Marshall Cavendish Corporation, 2001.

Greene, Nick. "Space Station - The International Space Station: Springboard to Future Space Exploration." About.com, a part of The New York Times Company. 22 Jan. 2008 <http://space. about.com/cs/iss/a/iss.htm>.

Oberg, James. "International Space Station." World Book Online Reference Center. 2005. World Book, Inc. 5 Aug. 2007 <http://www.worldbookonline.com/wb/Article?id=ar279523>.

VOCABULARY

A Find each word in the reading on page 156. Look at the words around it to guess the meaning. Compare your answers with a partner.

Adjectives	Nouns			Verbs
enormous	astronaut	mission	space station	assemble
long-term	cosmonaut	module	specimen	enable
valuable	endeavor	satellite		orbit
	exploration	solar panel		launch

B Complete the sentences using the words from the box. Use the appropriate form of the word.

mission   enormous   satellite   module   solar panel   launch

1. The International Space Station is a _____*satellite*_____ that circles the Earth.

2. The _____ of the space station is to allow scientists to live in space.

3. The space station is a series of _____ put together piece by piece.

4. The space station gets its energy from the _____ that cover the top.

5. The first part of the space station was _____ in 1998.

6. The space station is so _____ that more than fifteen countries are helping to build and fund the project.

C Write sentences using eight of the vocabulary words. You can use more than one word in each sentence.

1. *The International Space Station enables astronauts and cosmonauts to live in space for long-term stays.*

2. _____

   _____

3. _____

   _____

4. _____

   _____

5. _____

   _____

6. _____

   _____

Adjective Clauses	
Relative Pronoun	**Example Sentence**
that	Since its beginning, the International Space Station has been an endeavor **that** has brought people together throughout the world.
which	The United States with Canada, Europe, and Japan planned to build a space station, **which** they would call "Freedom."
who	What this means is that the astronauts and cosmonauts **who** visit the space station conduct scientific experiments.

- Adjective clauses describe nouns.
- Relative pronouns, such as *that*, *which*, and *who*, usually begin adjective clauses. *Who* is used with people. *That* and *which* are used with things.
- Use a comma before the relative pronoun and after the adjective clause only if the information in the adjective clause is not essential or defining.
  The space station, which orbits the Earth, is enormous.
  We don't need the information in the adjective clause to understand the sentence.
- Don't use commas if the adjective clause is essential to understanding the sentence.
  The space station that the Russians made is gone.
  We need to know which space station is being described.

A **Complete the sentences with *who*, *which*, or *that*.**

1. Scientists _____<u>who</u>_____ work on the International Space Station believe that part of humankind's future is in space.

2. The space station, _____ is large and very well designed, allows astronauts to live in space for long periods of time.

3. Astronauts _____ live in the space station are trying to learn more about humans living in space.

4. Perhaps living in space is something _____ will some day be a reality.

5. In order to make space habitation a reality, the astronauts and cosmonauts _____ live on the ISS must learn how to live healthy lives in space.

6. Because the Russians had so much experience with space stations, they built the first module, _____ was the most important.

B Complete the sentences with an adjective clause. Use commas as necessary.

1. The astronauts and cosmonauts _who visit and live on the space station_ come from all over the world.

2. They live and work at the space station in a very small area, _____.

3. The modules _____ are not very big, but they are very well designed.

4. The space station _____ benefits not only the scientists but everyone on Earth.

5. You and your friends _____ can observe the space station.

6. If you look on the Internet, you will find a schedule of the ISS's path over your city _____.

ORGANIZATION

Main Idea and Details

Complete the outline with information from the reading on page 156.

Remember!
An **essay** has an introduction paragraph, body paragraphs, and a conclusion paragraph. Information essays often use a **main idea and details** organizational structure. This means that the introduction paragraph presents the main idea of the essay, usually in the thesis statement. Then each body paragraph contains details that support the main idea. Within each body paragraph, the main idea and details structure is also maintained. Each topic sentence presents the main or most important idea of the paragraph. All the other sentences in that paragraph support and explain the main idea. Finally, the conclusion paragraph restates the main idea of the essay.

The International Space Station

I. **Introduction**
  A. Main idea: **1.** _to understand the importance of the ISS_ _____
  Details: **2.** _____
         3. _____
         4. _____

II. **Body Paragraph I**
  A. Main idea: **5.** _____
  Details: **6.** _____
         7. _____
         8. _____

III. Body Paragraph II

    A. Main idea: **9.** _____

    Details: **10.** _____

            11. _____

            12. _____

IV. Body Paragraph III

    A. Main idea: **13.** _____

    Details: **14.** _____

            15. _____

            16. _____

V. Conclusion

    A. Main idea summarized: **17.** _____

    Details: **18.** _____

            19. _____

            20. _____

WRITING STRATEGIES

Varying Sentence Structure

Label the following sentences as *simple*, *compound*, or *complex*.

1. Engineers and designers from all over the world have helped to build the space station modules.
   _____simple_____

2. One hatch connects to Zarya, and the others will connect to other modules.
   _____

3. Solar panels give the station its electricity. _____

Remember!

Sentence structure is how sentences are put together. To make your writing more interesting, vary the sentence structure. Sentences can be simple, compound, or complex.

Simple Sentences
A simple sentence has one complete thought, or independent clause:
Astronauts conduct science experiments.

Compound Sentences
A compound sentence has two simple sentences put together, usually with a comma and a connecting word such as: *and, but , or, for, so,* and *yet*:

One hatch connects to Zarya, <u>and</u> the others will connect to other modules.

Complex Sentences
A complex sentence has an independent clause and one or more dependent clauses. Remember that a dependent clause is an incomplete thought. It *depends* on the independent clause to make sense:

The United States stopped all space flights until it could be sure they would be safe.

4. When the space station was ready to be inhabited, its first crew included an American astronaut and two Russian cosmonauts. _____

5. In 2001, the United States ran out of money for the space station, so NASA decided to stop building new modules for the space station. _____

6. Then on February 1, 2003, the American space shuttle Columbia crashed. _____

7. All seven crewmembers died. _____

8. The United States stopped all space flights until it could be sure they would be safe. _____

WRITING CONVENTIONS

Using Colons

The sentences below are not punctuated correctly. Colons are missing. Re-write the sentences and add the colons where they belong.

> **Remember!**
> A colon is a punctuation mark that looks like two periods, one on top of the other, like this (:). Use a colon:
> - after the greeting in a business letter
>   *Dear Mr. Sanchez:*
> - between the parts of a number that tells the time
>   *11:45*
> - to formally introduce an explanation, a statement or question, or a quotation
>   *Frank Culbertson shared his thoughts about the ISS: "I believe what's going to come out of this. . . ."*
> - to introduce a list of words, phrases, or sentences
>   *The countries involved in the ISS are numerous: USA, Russia, Canada, Japan, European Union, etc.*

1. Dear Dr. Foale *Dear Dr. Foale:* _____

2. I would like to ask for your help on an essay I am writing. I need tutors for all my classes science, math, English, and social studies.

   _____

3. This month in class, we are studying the following subjects space stations, satellites, and scientific experiments in space.

   _____

4. I really respect what you said about working on the ISS "You just kind of get into this mechanical mode of thinking things through and trying to figure out what to do next."

   _____

5. If you could e-mail me back before 1130 tomorrow morning, that would be great!

   _____

Information Essay

An **information essay** is a nonfiction text, usually five or more paragraphs long. This kind of essay explains a topic that the writer has researched. The introduction paragraph introduces the main idea of the essay, defines any important terms, and gives any important background information. The body paragraphs each explain one detail that supports the main idea. Within each body paragraph, there are examples that support the detail. The conclusion paragraph summarizes the main idea and details of the first paragraph.

  A **Read.** Read Sonali's information essay about science experiments in space.

Experiments in Space

by Sonali Patel

Since the beginning of time, humans have made observations about and conducted experiments on their world. Experimenting is how humans have learned about the world around them. Today, we continue to learn about our world through experiments. However, now "our world" is the universe. When people conduct experiments in space, they understand the universe better. Because there is little gravity in space, different amounts of radiation, and different magnetic fields, space science allows us to know more than we can learn on Earth. Scientists in space have studied in nearly all fields of science. However, the most common fields of study in space are medicine, technology, and earth sciences.

Space scientists study the human body, animals, and microorganisms in order to better understand medicine. Astronauts and cosmonauts living in space stations study their own bodies to see how space affects them. Nearly every organ has been studied extensively in space. There have been experiments on the effects of low gravity on the spine, the feet, and even individual cells. Scientists have studied how space radiation affects the kidneys, the liver, and the heart. Scientists study how people sleep, exercise, and eat in space. They try to discover the best ways to keep astronauts healthy in space. Finally, space scientists have studied diseases such as cancer, cold viruses, and the production of antibodies in space (Wilson). These studies help scientists develop new medicines for people back on Earth who suffer from disease.

In order to conduct these experiments in space, engineers and scientists have had to develop technology for space science. First, they developed shuttles to take them into space. Then they developed space stations where they could stay and set up experiments. Finally, scientists and engineers designed tools to benefit experiments, space travel, and even people on Earth. They invented machines that test gravity so they know just how much or how little gravity there is in different parts of space. They invented solar equipment to be used in space and on Earth. They also had to invent specific tools like soldering equipment to be able to repair and build the technological devices in space (Wilson).

By far, the most studied subject in space is the Earth. More than 300,000 pictures have been taken of the Earth from the International Space Station (Wilson). Space scientists study

---

natural disasters happening on Earth, such as volcanoes, hurricanes, forest fires, droughts, and floods. They study human effects on the Earth, such as development and use of land and population effects (Dyson). From space, the Earth can be observed and recorded so that we can learn how best to care for it.

Humans have always conducted experiments to help us understand our world, and now we can learn even more about our bodies, machines, and the Earth through space science experiments. Scientists and engineers who work in space help us learn more about medicine, technology, and the Earth. Their discoveries benefit science, space travel, and all of us on Earth.

Source:
Dyson, Marianne J. <u>Space Station Science</u>. New York: Scholastic, 1999.
Wilson, Jim. "International Space Station." NASA. 14 Jan. 2008. 2 Feb. 2008 <http://www.nasa.gov/mission_pages/station/science/experiments/Expedition.html#16>.

B Re-read Sonali's essay on science experiments in space on page 162. Label each picture below with a brief summary of the paragraph it shows. The first has been done for you.

I.

Humans have conducted science experiments since the beginning of time. They help us understand our world.

II.

_____

_____

_____

_____

_____

III.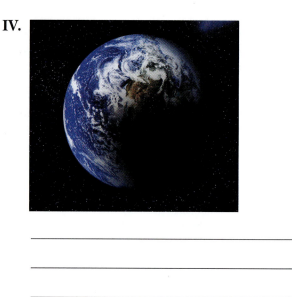

IV.

_____

_____

_____

_____

_____

_____

_____

_____

_____

_____

STEP-BY-STEP WRITING

Purpose: Research and Present a Topic

WRITING PROMPT

Write an information essay about a topic that you have researched. Share the essay with your teacher and classmates.

 **Prompt Checklist**

❑ I read the task carefully.
❑ I understood the form, audience, topic, and purpose of the prompt.

STEP 1 Pre-write

A Look at Sonali's list of possible topics. Make your own list.

Sonali's List of Topics

The origins of Karate

The history of the tomato

⟨Space experiments⟩

How silk is made

The ecology of vernal pools

B After you decide on your topic, read several books, magazine and newspaper articles, and Web sites about it. These are called **sources**. You should have at least two sources for your information essay.

- One source can be from the Internet; the other should be print material.
- Read the source thoroughly. Then read it again slowly, while taking notes on index cards.
- Write the source and page number at the top of the index card. Then, record important information on the index card.
- Include a main idea and the details that support it. You can write phrases and key words when taking notes.

Source: Dyson, Marianne J. Space Station Science. New York: Scholastic,

1999. p. 107

Astronauts study Earth.

study population and land use/development.

STEP 2 Organize

Look at Sonali's outline. Make your own outline for the topic you chose and information you found.

Sonali's Outline

Title: Experiments in Space

I. Introduction

A. Main idea: The most common fields of study in space are:

Details: 1. medicine

2. technology

3. earth sciences

II. Body Paragraph 1

A. Main idea: Space scientists study the human body, animals, and microorganisms to better understand medicine.

Details: 1. low gravity on all parts of the body

2. space radiation on body of humans and animals

3. diseases and viruses

III. Body Paragraph 2

A. Main idea: In order to conduct these experiments in space, engineers and scientists have had to develop technology for space science.

Details: 1. space ships

2. space stations

3. technology like welding tools

IV. Body Paragraph 3

A. Main idea: By far the most studied subject in space is the Earth.

Details: 1. natural disasters

2. human effects on the earth

V. Conclusion

A. Main idea summarized: Now we can learn even more about our bodies, machines, and the Earth through space science experiments.

STEP 3 Draft and Revise

A **Practice.** **Look at Sonali's first draft. How can she improve it? Answer the questions.**

First Draft
Experiments in Space
by Sonali Patel

(1) Since the beginning of time, humans have made observations about and conducted experiments on their world. (2) Experimenting is how humans have learned about the world around them.
(3) Today, we continue to learn about our world through experiments.
(4) However, now "our world" is the universe. (5) People understand the universe better. (6) Because there is little gravity in space, different amounts of radiation, and different magnetic fields, space science allows us to know more than we can learn on Earth.
(7) Scientists in space have studied in nearly all fields of science.
(8) However, the most common fields of study in space are medicine, technology, and earth sciences.

(9) Space scientists study the human body, animals, and microorganisms in order to better understand medicine. (10) Astronauts and cosmonauts living in space stations study their own bodies to see how space affects them. (11) Nearly every organ has been studied extensively in space.
(12) There have been experiments on the effects of low gravity on the spine, the feet, and even individual cells. (13) Scientists have studied how space radiation affects the kidneys, the liver, and the heart.
(14) They try to discover the best ways to keep astronauts healthy in space. (15) Finally, space scientists have studied diseases such as cancer, cold viruses, and the production of antibodies in space (Wilson).
(16) These studies help scientists develop new medicines for people back on Earth who suffer from disease.

(17) In order to conduct these experiments in space, engineers and scientists have had to develop technology for space science.
(18) First, they developed shuttles to take them into space.
(19) Then they developed space stations where they could stay and set up experiments. (20) Finally, scientists and engineers designed tools to benefit experiments, space travel, and even people on Earth. (21) They invented machines who test gravity so they know just how much or how little gravity there is in different parts of space. (22) They invented

solar equipment to be used in space and on earth. (23) They also had to invent specific tools like soldering equipment to be able to repair and build the technological devices in space (Wilson).

(24) More than 300,000 pictures have been taken of the Earth from the International Space Station (Wilson). (25) Space scientists study natural disasters happening on Earth, such as volcanoes, hurricanes, forest fires, droughts, and floods. (26) They study human effects on the Earth, such as development and use of land and population effects (Dyson). (27) From space, the Earth can be observed and recorded so that we can learn now best to care for it.

(28) Humans have always conducted experiments to help us understand our world. (29) Now we can learn even more about our bodies, machines, and the Earth through space science experiments. (30) Scientists and engineers that work in space help us learn more about medicine, technology and the Earth. (31) Their discoveries benefit science, space travel, and all of us on Earth.

1. How can Sonali rewrite sentence 5 to make it complex?
   A When people conduct experiments in space, they understand the universe better.
   B People, scientists, and astronauts conduct experiments in space.
   C To our benefit, people conduct and study experiments in space.
   D People and astronauts conduct and study experiments in space.

2. To what paragraph should Sonali add this detail? Scientists study how people sleep, exercise, and eat in space.
   A Paragraph 1
   B Paragraph 2
   C Paragraph 3
   D Paragraph 4

3. How can Sonali correct sentence 21?
   A Change *who* to *whose*.
   B Change *who* to *whom*.
   C Change *who* to *who's*.
   D Change *who* to *that*.

4. Which sentence should Sonali add to the beginning of paragraph 4?
   A Medicine is an important study in space.
   B By far the most studied subject in space is the Earth.
   C The Earth looks beautiful from space.
   D Let's keep the Earth, our home, beautiful.

5. How can sentences 28 and 29 be rewritten to be a compound sentence?
   A Humans have always conducted experiments to help us understand our world, and now we can learn even more about our bodies, machines, and the Earth through space science experiments.
   B Humans have always conducted experiments. This helps us understand our world. We can learn even more about our bodies, machines, and the Earth through space science experiments.
   C Space science experiments help us understand our world.
   D Experiments help us understand our bodies, machines, the Earth, and our whole world.

B **Draft.** Write a first draft of your information essay. Use your notes from Steps 1 and 2.

C **Revise.** Read your first draft. How can you improve it? Look at the revision checklist. Revise your writing.

STEP 4 Edit

A **Practice.** Read the sentences. Choose the best substitute for the underlined words. If the sentence is correct, choose "Make no change."

1. Dear Dr. <u>Armstrong</u>
   A armstrong
   Ⓑ Armstrong:
   C armstrong:
   D Make no change.

2. I am writing to ask you about the International Space <u>Solar</u>.
   A Station
   B Panel
   C Module
   D Make no change.

3. I have read that astronauts conduct experiments in the following <u>areas:</u> <u>medicine</u>, technology, and Earth studies.
   A areas" medicine
   B areas; medicine
   C areas, medicine
   D Make no change.

4. The scientists, who live on the space station study their own bodies.
   A scientists, who,
   B scientists, that
   C scientists who
   D Make no change.

5. They also study animals' <u>bodies which</u> can be easier to observe.
   A bodies, which
   B bodies, that,
   C bodies who
   D Make no change.

6. I have several questions for <u>you 1.</u> Are all astronauts scientists?
   A you 1:
   B you: 1.
   C you 1.:
   D Make no change.

7. If you leave Earth at <u>1.45</u> PM, what time do you arrive on the ISS?
   A 1,45
   B 1 and 45
   C 1:45
   D Make no change.

8. Do astronauts get dizzy from <u>enabling</u> around in circles?
   A launching
   B orbiting
   C assembling
   D Make no change.

B **Edit.** Re-read your draft from Step 3. Look at the editing checklist. Edit your writing.

C **Peer Edit.** Exchange drafts with a partner. Tell your partner what you like about the draft. Look at the editing checklist. Tell your partner how to improve the draft.

✔ Editing Checklist

me	my partner	
☐	☐	used capital letters correctly
☐	☐	used colons correctly
☐	☐	punctuated adjective clauses correctly
☐	☐	used vocabulary correctly

STEP 5 Publish

Rewrite your information essay in your best handwriting or use a computer. Look at Sonali's essay on page 163 for ideas. Present your information essay to the class.

TECHNOLOGY

Using a Computer to Research a Topic

- First, ask yourself research questions about your topic, using *how, why, where, when, who,* and *what*. Try to ask at least one question with each word.

- Then begin your research. Go to your favorite search engine. Type your topic in quotes. Click search.

- To choose appropriate and reliable Web sites, choose *.gov* sites first. If none are available, analyze the *.org, .edu,* and *.com* sites. Ask yourself, "Does the information seem reliable? Can I find it at another Web site? Does the person who wrote the Web site have good credentials?" Try to use only the Web sites that are run by reliable organizations and not individuals.

- Take notes on index cards as you do with book sources. Be sure to cite your sources carefully and thoroughly.

GROUP WRITING

Work in a group to write about one of these topics. Follow the steps below.

1. Choose your topic.
2. Discuss and record information.
3. Do research, if you need to.
4. Write a first draft.
5. Revise and edit the draft with your group.
6. Present your group's essay to the class.

Topic 1

Write a persuasive essay about something you strongly believe in. Use an anecdote or story, examples, and facts to argue your point.

Topic 2

Write an information essay on a topic that interests you. Read about the topic in at least two sources. Explain the topic with examples and supporting information.

TIMED WRITING

Choose one writing prompt. Complete the writing task in 45 minutes.

WRITING PROMPT 1

Write a five-paragraph persuasive essay about something you strongly disagree with. State your reasons for disagreeing with the topic. Provide stories, examples, and facts to support your opinions.

Test Tip

Formal Tone! Remember that when you write an essay, you use a formal tone. Your sentences have standard structure. You do not use contractions, exclamation points, or slang. You use precise vocabulary.

WRITING PROMPT 2

Write an information essay about something you do not know much about. After you choose a topic, read about it in at least two sources. Explain what you discovered, giving facts and other important information.

SELF-CHECK

Think about your writing skills. Check (✔) the answers that are true.

1. I understand. . .
   ❏ volunteer words.
   ❏ space words.

2. I can correctly. . .
   ❏ sort out reasons.
   ❏ use analogies, anecdotes, and evidence to support an argument.
   ❏ vary sentences for interest.

3. I can correctly use. . .
   ❏ modals.
   ❏ the future conditional tense.
   ❏ adjective clauses.

4. I can correctly use. . .
   ❏ words that signal opinion.
   ❏ colons.

5. I can organize my writing. . .
   ❏ point by point.
   ❏ by main idea and supporting details.

6. I can write to. . .
   ❏ argue a point.
   ❏ inform.

ARTICLES

Articles (p. 124)

An **article** is *a*, *an*, or *the*. The article *the* identifies something or someone definite. If you can answer the question *which one?* use *the.* Use *a* or *an* to talk about a nonspecific thing. Use *an* before nouns that start with a vowel sound. Use *a* before other nouns.

Article	Rule	Example
a, an	before general, singular count nouns use *a* before consonants use *an* before vowels	A conflict is **a** disagreement between two or more people. Tran and Marta made **an** agreement.
the	before specific nouns when there is only one	Usually, **the** disagreement makes one of the people, or disputants, feel that his or her needs or interests are threatened.

DEMONSTRATIVES

Demonstrative Adjectives and Pronouns (p. 75)

Demonstratives are the words *this*, *that*, *these*, and *those*. They're used as adjectives before nouns or as pronouns or replacements for nouns.

Demonstrative Adjective	Demonstrative Pronoun
These children are in second grade.	**This** means they're in Mrs. Lopez's class.

PREPOSITIONS

Prepositions (p. 6)

Prepositions tell **where**, **when**, and **how** something happens. Usually a noun follows a preposition.

Prepositional phrases are made up of: **preposition + noun = prepositional phrase**

Common Prepositions				
about	before	by	in	through
above	behind	during	into	to
across	below	except	of	under
around	beside	for	on	with
at	between	from	over	without

Prepositional Phrases for Location (p. 6)

Use a prepositional phrase to tell where something is located

Where?	on Elm Street	at Oak Street Park	across from Room 21

SENTENCES

Compound Sentences with Conjunctions (p. 23)

A **compound sentence with a conjunction** is formed when two separate sentences or independent clauses are combined using a conjunction, such as *or*, *and,* or *but*.

Compound Sentences with Conjunctions			
Sentence or Independent Clause	**Sentence or Independent Clause**	**Conjunction**	**Sentence**
I wanted to go shopping.	I had to go to work.	but	I wanted to go shopping, but I had to go to work.
I have a Bachelor's degree in English.	I have a Master's degree in elementary education.	and	I have a Bachelor's degree in English, and I have a Master's degree in elementary education.

Sentences with Adjective Clauses with *That, Which*, and *Who* (p. 41, 158)

Adjective clauses describe nouns. They cannot stand alone as a sentence. Relative pronouns like *that*, *which*, and *who* are used with adjective clauses.

Sentences with Adjective Clauses	
Relative Pronoun	**Sample Sentence**
who	Mrs. Flannery is the teacher who taught my class.
which	I plan to visit Japan, which is where my grandparents came from.
that	Apple pies made with apples that are grown in Washington are delicious.

Complex Sentences (p. 56)

Use a **complex sentences** to combine two or more clauses. By joining the clause into a complex sentence, the sentence is clearer.

Independent clauses are complete sentences. **Dependent clauses** are not complete sentences. Join the clauses with words such as **because** and **when**. Use a comma after the dependent clause when it is at the beginning of the sentence.

Complex Sentences		
Dependent Clause	**Independent Clause**	**Sentence**
Because she was tired,	She fell asleep on the couch.	Because she was tired, she fell asleep on the couch.
When they heard the noise,	They turned around and saw the truck.	When they heard the noise, they turned around and saw the truck.

Parallel Structure (p. 57)

Use **parallel structures** to join two or more nouns or **noun phrases** or verbs or verb **phrases** in a sentence.

A **verb phrase** is a verb joined with another word or words in a sentence. If a sentence has more than one **verb phrase**, the verbs must all agree or have the same form.

A **noun phrase** is a noun joined with another word or words in a sentence. If a sentence has more than one **noun phrase** together, the nouns must all agree or be the same form.

Parallel Structures	
Verb Phrase Agreement	**Noun Phrase Agreement**
She **worked** hard and **finished** her project.	Pets need **lots of food** and **lots of exercise**.
The leader **lead** the projects, **kept** us focused, and **worked** hard.	I admire her for her **work, dedication,** and **success**.

Complex Sentences with *If* Clauses (p. 124)

Use *if* clauses in **future conditionals** to talk about something that you think will happen in that situation. Use *will* in the **independent clause**.

Complex Sentences with *if* Clauses	
Dependent Clause (Condition)	**Independent Clause (Result)**
If I win the contest,	I will be happy.
If endangered animals lose their habitat,	they will die out.

If the *if clause* comes at the beginning of the sentence, place a comma after the *if clause.* Example: *If* it rains tomorrow, I will stay home.

If the *if clause* comes at the end of the sentence, do not use a comma. Example: I will stay home *if* it rains tomorrow.

VERBS

Simple Present Tense (p. 6)

Use the **simple present tense** to tell about an action that is true now or that generally happens.

Simple Present Tense with *be*	
Affirmative	**Negative**
I **am** from China.	I **am not** from Japan.
You **are** young.	You **are not** old.
Francisco **is** a student.	She **is not** a student.
My mother and I **are** at home.	We **are not** at school.
Tom and Tim **are** in Los Angeles.	They **are not** in New York City.

Simple Past Tense (p. 6, 22)

Use the **simple past tense** of a verb to tell about an action that happened in the past.

Simple Past Tense with *be*	
Affirmative	**Negative**
I **was** at the game.	I **was not** at the mall.
You **were** hungry before lunch.	You **were not** hungry after lunch.
Francisco **was** tired on Sunday night.	He **was not** tired on Saturday night.
We **were** on a bus yesterday.	We **were not** on a plane yesterday.
You **were** my classmates last year.	You **were not** my neighbors last year.
They **were** busy on Saturday morning.	They **were not** busy on Saturday night.

Simple Past Tense with Regular Verbs	
Affirmative	**Negative**
Francisco **helped** Maria.	Maria **did not help** her mother.
I **lived** in Haiti last year.	I **did not live** in Houston last year.
They **studied** on Sunday afternoon.	They **did not study** on Saturday night.
The Garcia family **shopped** for food.	The Garcia family **did not shop** for clothes.

Rules for Simple Past Tense		
IF...	**THEN...**	**Example**
If the verb ends in a **consonant**	then add **ed.**	help → help**ed**
If the verb ends in **e**	then add **d.**	live → live**d**
If the verb ends in **consonant** + **y**	then change **y** to **i** and add **ed.**	study → stud**ied**
If the verb ends in **vowel** + **consonant**	then double the consonant and add **ed.**	shop → shop**ped**

Past Tense of Irregular Verbs (p. 22)

Irregular verbs have special forms and are best memorized.

Past Tense of Irregular Verbs					
Base Form	**Simple Past Tense**	**Base Form**	**Simple Past Tense**	**Base Form**	**Simple Past Tense**
be	was/were	forget	forgot	ride	rode
become	became	get	got	ring	rang
begin	began	give	gave	run	ran
break	broke	go	went	say	said
bring	brought	grow	grew	see	saw
buy	bought	have	had	sell	sold
catch	caught	hear	heard	send	sent
choose	chose	hold	held	sing	sang
come	came	hurt	hurt	sit	sat
cost	cost	keep	kept	sleep	slept
cut	cut	know	knew	speak	spoke
do	did	leave	left	spend	spent
drink	drank	let	let	stand	stood
drive	drove	light	lit	take	took
eat	ate	lose	lost	teach	taught
fall	fell	make	made	tell	told
feel	felt	meet	met	think	thought
fight	fought	pay	paid	wear	wore
find	found	put	put	win	won
fly	flew	read	read	write	wrote

Infinitives and Gerunds (p. 56)

Infinitives are the *to* form of a verb. **Gerunds** are nouns made from a verb by adding *ing*.

Verb	Infinitive	Gerund
read	to read	reading
write	to write	writing

Present Continuous Tense (p. 42)

The **present continuous tense** tells about an action happening right now.

Use **be** and a main verb. Add **ing** to the end of the verb.

Present Continuous Tense

Affirmative	Negative
I **am eating** right now.	I **am not eating** right now.
You **are reading** right now.	You **are not reading** right now.
He **is writing** right now.	He **is not writing** right now.
We **are dancing** right now.	We **are not dancing** right now.
They **are running** right now.	They **are not running** right now.

Past Continuous Tense (p. 22)

Use the **past continuous tense** to talk about an action that was in progress at a specific time in the past.

Past Continuous Tense

Affirmative	Negative
I **was writing** a letter.	I **was not doing** homework.
Jennifer **was laughing**.	She **was not crying**.
They **were eating** a piece of cake.	They **were not eating** a slice of pie.

Present Tense vs. Present Continuous Tense (p. 41)

Present Tense vs. Present Continuous Tense

Present Tense Form	Present Continuous Tense Form	Sentence with Present Continuous
write	am writing	I am writing to inform you of my concerns.
offer	are offering	The lunches that you are offering are inadequate.

Passive Voice (p. 90)

Use the **passive voice** to focus on the result of an action, not the person who does the action.

Tense	The Passive Voice
Simple Present	Candy **is (not) sold** at school. Our photos **are (not) found** on the Internet.
Simple Past	The actor **was (not) admired** wherever he went. New software **was (not) developed** for this computer.

The subject of a passive verb corresponds to the object of an active verb.

Active Voice	Passive Voice
object Our school **performs** plays.	*subject* Plays **are performed** by our school.

Present Perfect Tense (p. 74, 91)

Use the **present perfect** to connect the past and the present. Use **have/has** + the **past participle** to make the **present perfect**. For most verbs, the past participle is the same as the simple past form. However, there are many verbs that have irregular past participles.

Present Perfect Tense	
Affirmative	**Negative**
I **have enjoyed** working with children.	I **have not worked** with adults.
She **has visited** New York this year.	She **has not visited** Atlanta, Georgia.
We **have eaten** Chinese food before.	We **have not eaten** Thai food.

Use **for** and **since** with the present perfect. Use **for** + a period of time. Use **since** + a point in time.

I have lived here for two years.

She has lived here since June 1st.

Regular Verbs			Irregular Verbs		
Present	**Past**	**Past Participle**	**Present**	**Past**	**Past Participle**
fix	fixed	fixed	be	was/were	been
live	lived	lived	come	came	come
talk	talked	talked	drink	drank	drunk
walk	walked	walked	get	got	gotten

Past Perfect Tense (p. 108)

Use the **past perfect** to talk about actions that happened before something else happened in the past. use: *had* (simple past of *have*) + past participle of the verb to make the **past perfect**.

Past Perfect Tense	
Affirmative	**Negative**
Jennifer **had walked** across town.	Jason **had not walked** across town.
She **had needed** to buy some fruit.	He **had not needed** to buy some fruit.

Linking Verbs (p. 74)

Use a **linking verb** to connect the subject of the sentence with a noun or adjective. Linking verbs do not show action.

Linking Verbs									
the *be* verbs			other common linking verbs						
am	is	are	appear	become	feel	get	grow	sit	look
was	were	been	prove	remain	seem	smell	sound	taste	turn

Modals (p. 142)

Use a **modal verb** to help the verb give more information.

Modal Verbs		
Purpose	**Affirmative**	**Negative**
ability	You **can** take the bus.	You **can not** take the train.
necessity	You **must** be careful when you cross the street.	You **must not** run.
recommendation	You **should** stay on Grand Street.	You **should not** go past the market.

Future Conditionals (p. 143)

Use the **future conditional** to express what will or may happen in the future if certain conditions are met. The future conditional tense is often used with *if/when* clauses.

Examples:

If I study a lot now, I will pass the test.

When I go to the library, I will borrow four books.

The football team will win many games if they practice hard.

The drama club will perform in a show when it's near the end of the school year.

CITATION GUIDE

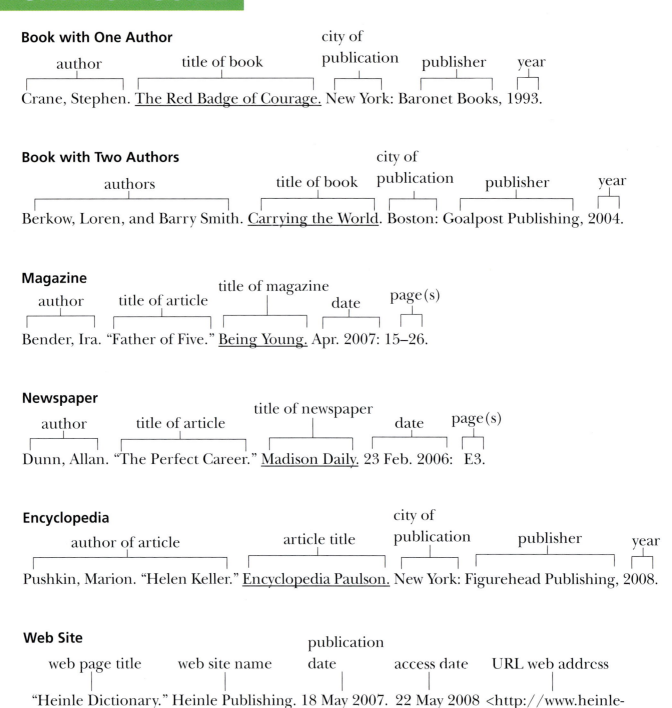

Book with One Author

author — Crane, Stephen.
title of book — The Red Badge of Courage.
city of publication — New York:
publisher — Baronet Books,
year — 1993.

Crane, Stephen. The Red Badge of Courage. New York: Baronet Books, 1993.

Book with Two Authors

authors — Berkow, Loren, and Barry Smith.
title of book — Carrying the World.
city of publication — Boston:
publisher — Goalpost Publishing,
year — 2004.

Berkow, Loren, and Barry Smith. Carrying the World. Boston: Goalpost Publishing, 2004.

Magazine

author — Bender, Ira.
title of article — "Father of Five."
title of magazine — Being Young.
date — Apr. 2007:
page(s) — 15–26.

Bender, Ira. "Father of Five." Being Young. Apr. 2007: 15–26.

Newspaper

author — Dunn, Allan.
title of article — "The Perfect Career."
title of newspaper — Madison Daily.
date — 23 Feb. 2006:
page(s) — E3.

Dunn, Allan. "The Perfect Career." Madison Daily. 23 Feb. 2006: E3.

Encyclopedia

author of article — Pushkin, Marion.
article title — "Helen Keller."
city of publication — Encyclopedia Paulson. New York:
publisher — Figurehead Publishing,
year — 2008.

Pushkin, Marion. "Helen Keller." Encyclopedia Paulson. New York: Figurehead Publishing, 2008.

Web Site

web page title — "Heinle Dictionary."
web site name — Heinle Publishing.
publication date — 18 May 2007.
access date — 22 May 2008
URL web address — <http://www.heinle-publishing.com>.

"Heinle Dictionary." Heinle Publishing. 18 May 2007. 22 May 2008 <http://www.heinle-publishing.com>.

STUDENT WRITING RUBRIC

Use this rubric to evaluate a peer's writing. Add your own criteria at the end of the list. Look at the score chart. Then, write a score next to each sentence. Add comments.

Score		Meaning
5		I strongly agree.
4		I agree.
3		I have no opinion.
2		I disagree.
1		I strongly disagree.

Criteria	Score	Comments
1. Development of Ideas		
The author answered the prompt completely.		
The writing has a purpose or main idea.		
All the ideas connect to a main idea.		
The details support the main ideas.		
The author shows an understanding of the topic.		
2. Organization		
The writing has an introduction, a body, and a conclusion.		
The ideas are in a logical order.		
The paragraphs are well-organized.		
3. Voice		
The author's voice is original.		
The writing is interesting.		
The writing addresses the correct audience.		
4. Fluency and Focus		
The writing maintains focus.		
There are meaningful transitions between ideas.		
The sentences and paragraphs are clear and concise.		
There are different sentence types.		
5. Conventions		
The sentences use correct grammar.		
The words and phrases are specific and meaningful.		
The punctuation and capitalization are correct.		
The spelling is correct.		
The author cites sources correctly.		
6. Presentation		
The presentation is in the correct format.		
The author included a title, name, and date.		
The first line of every paragraph is indented.		
7. My Criteria		
-		
-		
Total		
÷ 25		
Grade (out of 5)		

What your grade means:

5	4	3	2	1
excellent	great	good	need more practice	incomplete

GLOSSARY

analogy, p. 145 An **analogy** is a comparison between two situations used to support one's opinion in a persuasive essay.

anecdotes, p. 145 An **anecdote** is a personal story used to support one's opinion in a persuasive essay.

biographical narrative, p. 27 A **biographical narrative** is a true story about someone's life, written by another person.

body paragraph, p. 7 **Body paragraphs** are the paragraphs between the introduction and the conclusion in an essay.

business letter forms, p. 42, 45 A **business letter** and its envelope have standard **forms** and styles for addresses.

capitalization, p. 127 When you capitalize, you make a letter uppercase. There are many rules for **capitalization**.

charts and graph, p. 93 **Charts and graphs** give information visually.

chronological order, p. 24 **Chronological order** is the order in which events actually happen in a story.

citing a source, p. 59 **Citing sources** means that at the end of a piece of writing, the author lists the sources that he or she referenced.

colon, p. 161 A **colon** is a punctuation mark that looks like two periods, one on top of the other, like this **:**

combining information with relative clauses, p. 110 You can **combine information** from two sentences to form one sentence. Use relative pronouns like *who, which,* and *that* before the second sentence.

comma, p. 10 A **comma** is a punctuation mark that can be used in many ways, but is mainly used for separating things. It looks like this **,**

compare, p. 43 To **compare** two things means to assess their similarities.

compare and contrast essay, p. 91, 94 A **compare and contrast essay** tells how two or more subjects are alike and different.

compare and contrast words, p. 43, 93 **Compare and contrast words** show that two topics are being compared or contrasted.

concluding sentence, p. 7 The **concluding sentence** ends the written work and tells what it means.

concluding paragraph, p. 7 The **concluding paragraph** is the last paragraph in an essay.

connecting word, p. 59 A **connecting word**, like *because, that, although, for, while, when, who,* joins ideas or sentences.

connecting ideas with transition words, p. 111 Writers **connect two ideas between sentences using a transition word** such as: *as a result, in fact, in other words, instead,* and *nevertheless.* Each word or phrase shows a certain relationship between the two pieces of information.

contrast, p. 43 To **contrast** two things means to assess their differences.

definition essay, p. 58, 60 A **definition essay** is a nonfiction text, usually three to five paragraphs long, and all about one term or idea. This kind of essay gives and explains the dictionary definition for the term. Then it either offers a traditional/nontraditional examination of the term or examples and explanations of the term.

definition with two examples, p. 58 A definition essay is often structured in a way in which the author gives and explains **two different examples of a definition** of a term.

descriptive essay, p. 11 A **descriptive essay** describes a person, place, or thing in such detail so that the reader can picture and understand it.

details, p. 159 **Details** give more information about a main idea.

draw conclusions, p. 77 Readers **draw conclusions** by making sensible decisions based on details or facts in a reading.

expository writing, p. 11 **Expository writing** explains a topic. An example of expository writing is a descriptive essay.

evidence, p. 145 **Evidence**, or facts, is used to support one's opinion in a persuasive essay.

five-paragraph essay, p. 76, 109 A **five-paragraph essay** has an introduction paragraph, three body paragraphs, and a conclusion paragraph.

general-to-specific essay, p. 76, 79 In a **general-to-specific essay**, the introduction gives and explains the generalization or general thought about the topic. Each body paragraph gives and explains a specific example of the generalization. The conclusion summarizes the examples and relates them back to the generalization.

inference, p. 25 When you make **inferences**, you guess using information that you know to arrive at a conclusion.

information essay, p. 162 An **information essay** is a nonfiction text, usually five or more paragraphs in length that explains a topic that the writer has researched.

information sheet, p. 17 An **information sheet** is a page of concise text and pictures about a subject.

introduction paragraph, p. 7 An **introduction paragraph** gives general, important information about the topic of an essay.

keyword search, p. 33, 51, 67, 85, 153 A **keyword search** is a search that uses a specific word or words to look up information on the Internet.

order of importance, p. 42 **Order of importance** means to give the most important information first.

parentheses, p. 59 **Parentheses** are punctuation marks used to enclose words or numbers and look like this ( ).

parenthetical citation, p. 59 Within an article, a **parenthetical citation** is used to document an external source of information. It includes the author's last name and the specific page number for the information cited. For example, (Anderson, 80).

main idea, p. 159 The **main idea** (or controlling idea) is the focus, central thought, or purpose of a paragraph.

letter of complaint, p. 42 A **letter of complaint** is a type of business letter that uses formal language to voice a concern and request a solution.

persuasive essay, p. 144, 146 A **persuasive essay** gives the writer's opinion and tries to convince the reader to agree with it.

process description essay, p. 125, 128 In a **process description essay**, or sequential essay, the introduction paragraph tells any steps you need to complete before beginning the process.

register, p. 43 The **register** is the writing style one uses.

relative clauses, p. 110 **Relative clauses** tell more about a noun in a sentence.

reported speech, p. 26 **Reported speech** tells what someone said and does not use quotes.

research a topic, p. 169 When you **research a topic**, you find information about it form a variety of sources.

response to literature, p. 111, 112 A **response to literature essay** is a nonfiction text, usually five or more paragraphs long. This kind of essay tells what the writer thinks about another piece of literature.

scenario, p. 125 A **scenario**, or a specific example, helps to explain a step in a process.

sensory adjective, p. 9 A **sensory adjective** is a descriptive word that appeals to one of the five senses.

INDEX

Grammar, Usage, and Mechanics

Organization

Reading

Technology

Vocabulary and Language

Writing

Writing Conventions

Writing Strategies